THE ULTIMATE
HOCKEY
CHALLENGE

This edition published in 2006

For AG City Wholesale Ltd

By Arcturus Publishing Limited
26/27 Bickels Yard, 151–153 Bermondsey Street,
London SE1 3HA

ISBN-13: 978-1-84193-408-2
ISBN-10: 1-84193-408-9

Printed in China

THE ULTIMATE HOCKEY CHALLENGE

THE BEST HOCKEY QUIZ BOOK EVER

John A. White

Capella

The *Ultimate Hockey Challenge* is a book by a hockey fan for all other hockey fans, young or old, no matter which team you support.

I have tried to make it like no other hockey quiz book out there, with questions that really test your knowledge of the game, and answers that offer surprising and fascinating facts about the sport we all love.

Rather than divide the book into questions about teams, or trophies, or player positions, I have organized these 1000 questions in a series of 63 quizzes that cover all aspects and eras of this magnificent game. This way all fans of any age can participate in each quiz.

There should truly be something for everyone in *The Ultimate Hockey Challenge*, with questions of all levels of difficulty. I hope you enjoy wrestling with these quizzes even half as much as I have enjoyed putting them together.

John A. White

QUIZ 1

1 Who was named the inaugural winner of the Conn Smythe Memorial Trophy as the most valuable player in the National Hockey League's Stanley Cup Playoffs?

2 Who are the last set of brothers to be selected to the NHL's First All-Star Team in the same season?

3 Who is the only player to lead the National Hockey League in goal scoring in seven different seasons?

4 Who is the only defenseman in NHL history to score more than 400 regular season goals in his career?

5 Name the franchise that holds the NHL record for the most consecutive appearances in the Stanley Cup Finals.

6 The Philadelphia Flyers of the 1990s featured a lethal forward line known as the "Legion of Doom". Name the members of this outstanding forward line.

7 Who coached the Toronto Maple Leafs to their last four Stanley Cup Championships?

8 For which Quebec Major Junior Hockey League team did both Vincent Lecavalier and Brad Richards play their major junior hockey?

9 Since the inception of the National Hockey League Entry Draft in 1963, the Toronto Maple Leafs have had the first overall pick only once. Name the player that the Leafs chose with their only first overall selection.

10 Who was the last goaltender to be voted the winner of the Calder Memorial Trophy as the NHL's rookie of the year?

11 Name the two cities that were granted National Hockey League franchises when the league expanded from 12 to 14 teams for the 1970-71 season.

12 Who is known simply as "Mr. Hockey"?

13 Name the only three players in NHL history to score more than 80 goals in a single regular season.

14 Who is the only member of the New Jersey Devils to win the James Norris Trophy as the NHL's best defenseman?

15 Who was the first European-trained player to win the Hart Memorial Trophy as NHL's most valuable player?

16 Who was the first player to win the Conn Smythe Memorial Trophy as the Stanley Cup Playoff's most valuable player, in consecutive years?

QUIZ 2

1 Name the two defensemen who scored at least 20 goals in a season, a record nine times during their NHL careers.

2 Who was the last member of the Montreal Canadiens to win the Art Ross Trophy as the NHL's leading point producer?

3 On May 15th, 1967, one of the most lopsided trades in NHL history occurred. The Boston Bruins sent Gilles Marotte, Pit Martin and Jack Norris to the Chicago Blackhawks in exchange for three superb players. Name the players obtained by the Bruins in this trade?

4 Name the only goaltender in NHL history to be selected to either the First or Second All-Star Team more than ten times.

5 With which World Hockey Association franchise did Mark Messier begin his professional hockey career?

6 Name the only player in NHL history to score at least 50 goals in a season nine consecutive times.

7 How many times have the Detroit Red Wings won the Stanley Cup?

8 What member of the Hockey Hall of Fame was bestowed with the nickname "Chief-Shoot-the-Puck"?

9 Name the only two players in hockey history to score at least 50 goals in a season in both the National Hockey League and the World Hockey Association.

10 The Pittsburgh Penguins have had the first overall selection in the NHL Entry Draft three times since the Draft's inception. Name the players that the Penguins chose with their number one picks.

11 Who was the leading scorer for Canada in the 1972 Canada-Russia Summit Series?

12 Name the four NHL teams that Wayne Gretzky played for during his incomparable career.

13 Who is the youngest player ever to be inducted into the Hockey Hall of Fame?

14 Who was the first player to win an Olympic gold medal and a Stanley Cup ring in the same year?

15 Who was the first European-born player selected first overall in the National Hockey League Entry Draft?

16 Who was the first goaltender to register over 400 regular season victories in the National Hockey League?

QUIZ 3

1 Who was the last member of the Detroit Red Wings to win the Calder Memorial Trophy as the NHL's rookie of the year?

2 Who holds the NHL single season record for the most shorthanded goals?

3 Name the members of the New York Rangers prolific scoring line known as the GAG Line.

4 Who is the only member of the Tampa Bay Lightning to win the Conn Smythe Memorial Trophy as the NHL's most valuable player in the Stanley Cup Playoffs?

5 In 1967, the National Hockey League expanded from 6 to 12 teams. Name the six teams to be granted expansion franchise in 1967.

6 Name the only man to win the Jack Adams Award as the National Hockey League's coach of the year, in consecutive seasons.

7 Name the only two defensemen in NHL history to record more than 1500 points in their careers?

8 Who holds the NHL record for the most shutouts in a season by a rookie goaltender?

9 In 1999, the National Hockey League introduced the Maurice "Rocket" Richard Trophy. The Richard Trophy is awarded to the player who leads the NHL in goal scoring during the regular season. Name the inaugural winner of the Richard Trophy?

10 Who was the last member of the Philadelphia Flyers to win the Hart Memorial Trophy as the National Hockey League's most valuable player?

11 Name the Hockey Hall of Fame defenceman who led the National Hockey League in penalty minutes an incredible eight years in succession.

12 For which Ontario Hockey League team did Doug Gilmour play his major junior hockey?

13 Who is the only player in NHL history to win the Art Ross, Hart and Lady Byng Trophies in consecutive seasons?

14 For which team did Borje Salming play the final game of his National Hockey League career?

15 Who was the first Russian trained player to be drafted first overall in the NHL Entry Draft?

16 The 1963-64 NHL First All-Star Team was dominated by the Chicago Blackhawks. Glenn Hall, Pierre Pilote, Stan Mikita, Ken Wharram and Bobby Hull were all selected to the NHL's first team. Who was the only non-Blackhawk to be selected to the NHL's First All-Star Team in 1963-64?

QUIZ 4

1 Who was the youngest player to capture the Conn Smythe Memorial Trophy as the most valuable player in the Stanley Cup Playoffs?

2 For what two National Hockey League teams did the legendary Don Cherry handle the coaching duties?

3 Name the youngest goaltender to appear in a National Hockey League game.

4 Who was the first member of the Philadelphia Flyers to score at least 50 goals in a single NHL season?

5 Wayne Gretzky scored 60 or more goals during a season five times in his incredible career. Name the only other player in NHL history to accomplish this amazing feat.

6 Who was the last member of the Boston Bruins to win the Art Ross Memorial Trophy as the NHL's leading scorer during the regular season?

7 Name the team that holds the National Hockey League record for the most victories in a single regular season.

8 Who is the only player in NHL history to score 3 shorthanded goals in a single regular season game?

9 Hockey Hall of Fame broadcaster Foster Hewitt called this diminutive center "Mr. Perpetual Motion". To whom was Hewitt referring?

10 Name the only two players in NHL history to record at least one point in over 40 consecutive games.

11 Who is the only member of the New York Rangers to win the Conn Smythe Memorial Trophy as the most valuable player in the Stanley Cup Playoffs?

12 Who was the first Finnish-born player to be inducted into the Hockey Hall of Fame?

13 In 1967, "Punch" Imlach, coach and general manager of the Toronto Maple Leafs, said of this player: "We are not going to lose to a Junior 'B' goalie!" Name the netminder Imlach was referring to.

14 In their inaugural season, who did the Buffalo Sabres select with the first pick of the National Hockey League Entry Draft?

15 Who was the last member of the Toronto Maple Leafs to win the Lady Byng Trophy as the NHL's most gentlemanly player?

16 The Detroit Red Wings of the 1950s featured perhaps the best forward line in the NHL of the decade. Name the three members of the Red Wings' famed "Production Line".

QUIZ 5

1 Who is the youngest player in NHL history to record at least 100 points in his rookie season?

2 Who holds the NHL record for the most penalty minutes in a single regular season?

3 Who was the last NHL goaltender to appear in a game without a mask?

4 Name the only two defensemen in NHL history to record as many as 90 assists in a single season.

5 Who was the last player to lead the National Hockey League in goal scoring in three consecutive seasons?

6 Who is the only player to record five assists in the National Hockey League's All-Star Game?

7 Name the legendary broadcaster who coined the phrases, "Savardian Spin a Rama" and "Cannonading Shot".

8 Name the four World Hockey Association organizations that became members of the National Hockey League for the 1979-80 season.

9 Who is the only member of the Pittsburgh Penguins to win the James Norris Trophy as the NHL's outstanding defenseman?

10 With which Ontario Hockey League team did Steve Yzerman play his major junior hockey?

11 On June 10th, 1957, the Boston Bruins and the Detroit Red Wings were involved in a trade that saw two future Hall of Fame members change teams. Name the players involved in this major trade.

12 Who was the first United States born player to score at least 50 goals in a single NHL season?

13 Name the NHL "tough guy" who went by nickname "Leapin' Lou".

14 Name the only two players in NHL history who have won the Hart Memorial Trophy as the NHL's most valuable player in at least three consecutive seasons.

15 Name the two members of the Toronto Maple Leafs who left the team to sign as unrestricted free agents with the Florida Panthers in the summer of 2005.

16 Name the only player in NHL history to score 30 or more goals in 15 consecutive seasons.

QUIZ 6

1 What was Gordie Howe's jersey number when he first entered the National Hockey League in 1946?

2 Best known as a member of the Boston Bruins, Cam Neely began his NHL career with what team?

3 Who played an incredible 884 consecutive NHL games as a member of the Chicago Blackhawks?

4 Who was the first goaltender to win the Vezina Trophy four years in succession?

5 Who was the first rookie in NHL history to score 50 goals in a single regular season?

6 Name the only two members of the New York Islanders to score five goals in a single NHL game.

7 From 1989 until 1991 the Quebec Nordiques had the first overall selection in the National Hockey League Entry Draft. Name the players that the Nordiques selected with the first pick of these three Drafts.

8 Who was the first winner of the James Norris Trophy as the NHL's outstanding defenseman?

9 Who was known simply as "Mr. Goalie"?

10 Who was the last member of the Boston Bruins to record at least 100 points in a single NHL season?

11 Who was the first Commissioner of the National Hockey League?

12 Who was the first defenseman to record 1000 points in his National Hockey League career?

13 Roger Crozier, Glenn Hall, Ron Hextall and Jean-Sebastien Giguere all won the Conn Smythe Memorial Trophy as the Stanley Cup Playoffs most valuable player despite the fact that their team lost in the Stanley Cup Finals. Name the only non-goaltender to capture the Conn Smythe Trophy, while playing for the losing team in the Stanley Cup Final.

14 Who is the only coach in NHL history to be behind the bench for over 700 victories with one team?

15 Name the members of the Montreal Canadiens defense corp who were known as "The Big Three".

16 The NHL record for assists in a season by a rookie stands at 70. Name the two players that share this record.

1 Who is the only NHL head coach to win the Jack Adams Award as the NHL's coach of the year three times?

2 Name the only member of the Colorado Avalanche to win the Art Ross Trophy as the National Hockey League's leading scorer.

3 Who is the only member of the Los Angeles Kings to win the Lester B. Pearson Award as the National Hockey League's most valuable player as selected by the National Hockey League Player Association?

4 The legendary Howie Morenz was given four nicknames during his magnificent NHL career. What were the nicknames that Morenz answered to?

5 Who is the only player in NHL history to win the Art Ross Trophy as the NHL's leading scorer and the Rocket Richard Trophy as the league's top goal scorer, in the same season?

6 Who is the Toronto Maple Leafs' all-time career point scoring leader?

7 Name the only two defensemen in National Hockey League history to be selected to the NHL's First All-Star Team ten or more times in their careers.

8 For which franchise did Hockey Hall of Fame member Tony Esposito play his first NHL game?

9 Who was the first American-born player to win the James Norris Trophy as the NHL's best defenseman?

10 Who holds the National Hockey League record for the fastest three goals in a single game?

11 Name the National Hockey League team that holds the record for the longest winning streak from the start of a season.

12 Who was known as "The Grate One"?

13 Who was the first player in National Hockey League history to record 100 points in a regular season?

14 Who holds the Chicago Blackhawks franchise record for the most games played as a Blackhawk?

15 Who was nicknamed "Sudden Death" for his overtime scoring prowess during the 1939 Stanley Cup Playoffs?

16 Who holds the NHL record for the most game winning goals in one Stanley Cup Playoffs campaign?

QUIZ 8

1 What was the name of the Pittsburgh franchise that was a member of the National Hockey League from 1925 until 1930?

2 Who scored the game winning goals for Canada in both game six and seven of the 1972 "Summit Series" against the Russians?

3 Name the NHL coach who saw his club lose in the Stanley Cup Final an incredible 12 times.

4 Who finished second in the National Hockey League scoring race a record five times during his career?

5 Who is the only member of the Boston Bruins to win the Conn Smythe Memorial Trophy as the Stanley Cup Playoff's most valuable player?

6 The Edmonton Oilers have had four players score 40 or more goals in the same season an amazing four times. Name the only other NHL team to accomplish this feat even once.

7 Who is the only member of the Pittsburgh Penguins to have his jersey number retired by the club?

8 Who was the first European-trained player to win the Art Ross Trophy as the NHL's leading scorer?

9 Who was the last goaltender to play every minute of every game for an entire NHL regular season schedule?

10 With which Ontario Hockey League team did Chris Pronger play his major junior hockey?

11 On June 29th, 1990, the Montreal Canadiens traded defenseman Chris Chelios and a second round draft pick to the Chicago Blackhawks. Who did the Habs receive from the Hawks to complete the deal?

12 Name the first defenseman in NHL history to win the Conn Smythe Memorial Trophy as the most valuable player in the Stanley Cup Playoffs.

13 Who was the coach of the United States Olympic Team when the Americans won the Olympic Gold Medal in hockey at the Winter Games in 1980?

14 Name the goaltending tandem that backstopped the Toronto Maple Leafs to the Stanley Cup Championship in 1967.

15 Who is the only member of the St. Louis Blues to win the Calder Memorial Trophy as the National Hockey League's rookie of the year?

16 Name the members of the Toronto Maple Leafs' magnificent forward line known as "The Kid Line".

QUIZ 9

1 Who was the last member of the Montreal Canadiens to score at least 50 goals in a single NHL regular season?

2 Wayne Gretzky led the National Hockey League in assists an amazing 16 times during his illustrious career. Only one other player has led the league in assists as many as five times. Name him.

3 Name the only member of the Los Angeles Kings to record at least eight points in a single NHL game.

4 Who holds the NHL record for the most games played by a goaltender in a single regular season?

5 On March 20th, 1996, the Vancouver Canucks traded Alek Stojanov to the Pittsburgh Penguins. Who did the Canucks receive from the Penguins to complete the trade?

6 Who was the first member of a 1967 expansion franchise to win the Hart Memorial Trophy as the NHL's most valuable player?

7 Name the only player in hockey history to score over 300 goals in both the National Hockey League and the World Hockey Association.

8 For which team did the controversial Don Cherry play his only game in the National Hockey League?

9 The record for shutouts by a goalkeeper in a single NHL season stands at 22. Who holds this seemingly unbreakable record?

10 Best known as a member of the Montreal Canadiens, with which NHL team did Doug Harvey play the final game of his marvelous career?

11 Name the two players who share the NHL record for the most points by a defenseman in a single game.

12 Who was the first winner of the Jack Adams Award as the National Hockey League's coach of the year?

13 Who was the first American-born player to record at least 100 points in a single NHL season?

14 What NHL goaltending great was dubbed "Jake the Snake"?

15 Since the inception of the National Hockey League Entry Draft, the Buffalo Sabres have had the first selection in the Draft only twice. Name the players that the Sabres selected with the first picks in the Drafts.

16 On February 13th, 1999, the final NHL game was played at Toronto's storied Maple Leaf Gardens. Who scored the last goal in the history of this fabled arena?

QUIZ 10

1 Who was the first member of the New York Rangers to score at least 50 goals in a single NHL season?

2 Name the only Soviet-trained player to score more than 70 goals in a single NHL season.

3 Who is the youngest player in NHL history to serve as a team captain?

4 With which World Hockey Association team did Gordie, Mark and Marty Howe make hockey history, by becoming the first father and sons to play together professionally?

5 With which Ontario Hockey League team did Eric Lindros play his major junior hockey?

6 Who is the only member of the Ottawa Senators to win the Calder Memorial Trophy as the NHL's rookie of the year?

7 Name the only two members of the Montreal Canadiens to win the Lady Byng Trophy as the NHL's most gentlemanly player, in the franchise's illustrious history.

8 What is the name of the trophy awarded to the playoff champions of the American Hockey League?

9 Who is the only member of the Los Angeles Kings to win the Hart Memorial Trophy as the NHL's most valuable player?

10 Who is the only player in NHL history to record at least 1000 career points and accumulate more than 3000 minutes in penalties?

11 Name the only player in NHL history to win the Maurice "Rocket" Richard Trophy as the NHL's leading goal scorer in back to back seasons.

12 Who was the last member of the Toronto Maple Leafs to reach the 50 goal plateau in a single NHL season?

13 Name the NHL goaltender who backstopped his club to a record ten overtime wins in a single Stanley Cup Playoff campaign.

14 Name the former Toronto Maple Leaf defenseman that went by the nickname "Howie".

15 Who was the first player to record a "Hat Trick"(3 goals) in the NHL All-Star Game?

16 Name the team that holds the record for the longest undefeated streak in National Hockey League history.

QUIZ 11

1 Who is the only member of the Calgary Flames to win the Conn Smythe Memorial Trophy as the NHL's most valuable player in the Stanley Cup Playoffs?

2 Who holds the NHL record for the most goals scored by a defenseman in a single game?

3 Who was voted as Canada's most outstanding hockey player of the first half of the 20th century?

4 On December 29th, 1979, the Colorado Rockies traded Pat Hickey and Wilf Paiement to the Toronto Maple Leafs. Name the two players that the Leafs sent to the Rockies to complete the trade.

5 Who was the last goalkeeper to win the Hart Memorial Trophy as the NHL's most valuable player?

6 Who won the Frank J. Selke Trophy as the NHL's best defensive forward the first four years that the Trophy was awarded?

7 Sometimes known as the "Trio Grande", this troika of New York Islanders led the team to four consecutive Stanley Cup Championships. Name the talented members of this Islander forward line.

8 Who was the last Toronto Maple Leaf to record his 1000th career point while a member of the team?

9 In what year did the Stanley Cup come under the control of the National Hockey League?

10 Who was the last member of the Chicago Blackhawks to win the Calder Memorial Trophy as the NHL's rookie of the year?

11 Name the only member of the Calgary Flames to score five goals in a single NHL game?

12 In 2005, the National Hockey League instituted the shootout to decide regular season games, after the five minute overtime period. Name the two teams that participated in the first NHL game to be decided by a shootout?

13 For what Western Hockey League team did Joe Sakic play the final two seasons of his major junior hockey career?

14 Who is the only member of the Toronto Maple Leafs to win the Conn Smythe Memorial Trophy as the NHL's most valuable player in the Stanley Cup Playoffs?

15 Who was the first European trained player to win the Calder Memorial Trophy as the NHL's rookie of the year?

16 Name the team that was granted an NHL franchise to begin the 1999-2000 season.

QUIZ 12

1 Name the only player in NHL history to receive ten penalties in a single game.

2 In March 1955, Maurice Richard was well on his way to winning the NHL scoring title. However, he was suspended for the final three games of the regular season, thus denying him the Art Ross Trophy. Who passed Richard in the NHL scoring race to claim the 1955 Art Ross Trophy?

3 Name the only member of the Edmonton Oilers to win the James Norris Memorial Trophy as the NHL's best defenseman.

4 Best known as a Boston Bruin, Johnny McKenzie was known by what nickname?

5 On February 6th, 1998, the Vancouver Canucks traded Trevor Linden to the New York Islanders. Name the players that the Canucks obtained from the Islanders to complete the trade?

6 Who is the only defenseman in National League history to win the Hart Memorial Trophy as the league's most valuable player four times in his career.

7 Name the only coach in NHL history to coach in five different decades.

8 Name the only two players in NHL history to score as many as five goals in a single game, during their rookie year in the league.

9 Who was the first player in NHL history to record at least 30 points in a single Stanley Cup Playoff campaign?

10 For which National Hockey League team did Doug Gilmour play the first game of his professional career?

11 Name the only goaltender in NHL history to win 40 or more games in his rookie season.

12 Who was the last member of the Montreal Canadiens to win the Calder Memorial Trophy as the NHL's top rookie?

13 How many times have the New York Rangers won the Stanley Cup?

14 Who holds the Philadelphia Flyers team record for the most points in a single NHL season?

15 Name the only two players in NHL history to score at least 20 goals in a season at least 20 times in their NHL careers.

16 Maurice Richard, Mike Bossy, Wayne Gretzky, Mario Lemieux and Brett Hull have all scored fifty goals in 50 games or less during a NHL regular season. Name the only two other players to accomplish this feat?

QUIZ 13

1 On March 20th, 1971, NHL history was made as two brothers faced each other as opposing goaltenders for the first time in league history. Name the goaltending brothers who took part in this historic game?

2 Who is the longest serving team captain in the history of the National Hockey League?

3 Who was the first member of the Toronto Maple Leafs to score at least 50 goals in an NHL regular season?

4 With which Western Hockey League team did Scott Niedermayer play his major junior hockey?

5 Who was the first defenseman in NHL history to record 500 points in his career?

6 Who is known simply as "The Dominator"?

7 The Detroit franchise in the National Hockey League became known as the Red Wings in the 1932-33 season. By what two names was the team previously known?

8 Who is the only coach of the Ottawa Senators to win the Jack Adams Award as the NHL's coach of the year?

9 Who holds the NHL record for the most goals scored by a rookie in one Stanley Cup Playoff year?

0 Who is sometimes referred to as "Mario Jr."?

1 In which Winter Olympic Games did the International Olympic Committee first permit teams to include professional players on their rosters?

2 Who was the last member of the Detroit Red Wings to win the Art Ross Memorial Trophy as the NHL's leading point producer?

3 Name the Hall of Fame goaltender who was sometimes referred to as "The China Wall".

4 Who was the first player in National Hockey League history to win four major awards in a single season?

5 The City of Vancouver was granted an NHL franchise in 1970. Who did the Canucks select with their first pick of the 1970 NHL Entry Draft?

6 Who was the first member of the Buffalo Sabres to score at least 50 goals in a single NHL season?

QUIZ 14

1 Name the only European-trained player to capture the Conn Smythe Trophy as the NHL's most valuable player in the Stanley Cup Playoffs.

2 Name the first US-born Collegiate player to be selected first overall in the NHL Entry Draft.

3 On October 11th, 1952, the Canadian Broadcasting Corporation began televising NHL games. Name the broadcaster who was the play-by-play voice in the first game televised on the CBC.

4 Who holds the National Hockey League record for the most penalty minutes by an individual in League history?

5 Name the Hall of Fame defenseman who was known as "The Edmonton Express".

6 Whose goal at 16:30 of the sixth overtime period ended the longest game in the history of the National Hockey League?

7 Who was the inaugural winner of Masterton Trophy awarded to the NHL player who best exemplifies perseverance and dedication to the game of hockey?

8 On October 18th, 2005, Paul Coffey became the fifth member of the Edmonton Oilers to have his sweater number retired by the team. Name the four other Oilers to have their jerseys retired.

9 Which NHL team holds the modern day record for the fewest losses in one NHL regular season?

10 Who was the first netminder to be selected first overall in the National Hockey League Entry Draft?

11 Name the former winner of the Calder Memorial Trophy as the NHL's rookie of the year who went by the nickname "The Eel", during his playing days.

12 Who is the only member of the Calgary Flames to score at least 50 goals in his rookie season in the NHL?

13 Who was the last member of the Toronto Maple Leafs to win the Hart Memorial Trophy as the NHL's most valuable player?

14 Name the arena in which the Chicago Blackhawks played their National Hockey League home games, from 1929 until 1994.

15 Name the four players in NHL history, to win the Art Ross Memorial Trophy as the league's leading scorer, at least four consecutive times.

16 Who holds the record for the most career points by a defenseman in the NHL All-Star games?

QUIZ 15

1 On July 23rd, 1957, the Detroit Red Wings traded two future Hall of fame members to the Chicago Blackhawks for Johnny Wilson, Forbes Kennedy, Bill Preston and Hank Bassen. Name the players that the Hawks acquired in this relatively one-sided deal.

2 The Montreal Canadiens franchise record for the most goals by a player in a single season stands at 60. Name the two players that share this team record.

3 Who was the last player to play an NHL game without a helmet?

4 Who coached the Philadelphia Flyers to back to back Stanley Cup Championships in 1975 and 1976?

5 During the 1943-44 NHL season , the Montreal Canadiens famed "Punch Line" was formed. Name the members of this prolific scoring line.

6 Name the two NHL franchises that merged in 1978, leaving the National Hockey League with just 17 teams.

7 Name the two members of the Colorado Avalanche who have won the Hart Memorial Trophy as the NHL's most valuable player.

8 On November 27th, 1960, Gordie Howe of the Detroit Red Wings became the first player in NHL history to record 1000 career points. Who was the next NHL player to tally 1000 points in his career?

9 Who was the last NHL netminder to win the Vezina Trophy as the league's outstanding goalkeeper in back to back seasons?

10 With which Western Hockey League team did Mike Modano play his major junior hockey?

11 Name the first player in NHL history to selected first overall in the NHL Entry Draft, to capture the Calder Memorial Trophy as the NHL's rookie of the year.

12 Name the player who scored the most regular season goals in the history of the World Hockey Association.

13 Name the four members of the New York Islanders who won the Conn Smythe Memorial Trophy as the Stanley Cup Playoffs' most valuable player.

14 Who holds the National Hockey League record for the most consecutive complete games played by a goaltender?

15 Who is the only member of the Los Angeles Kings to score at least 70 goals in a single NHL regular season?

16 Who was the first European-trained player to participate in a National Hockey League game?

QUIZ 16

1 The fastest overtime goal in Stanley Cup Playoff history was scored after only nine seconds of the first overtime period. Name the player who scored this record setting goal.

2 Who is the only coach of the Vancouver Canucks to win the Jack Adams Award as the NHL's coach of the year?

3 Name the two teams that participated in the first all American Stanley Cup Final.

4 Who was the last New York Rangers netminder to be selected to the NHL's First All-Star Team?

5 Name the Hall of Fame defenseman who was known as "Snowshoes".

6 In the 1983-84 season, Wayne Gretzky of the Edmonton Oilers established an NHL record by recording at least one point in 51 consecutive games. Who held the consecutive game scoring record prior to Gretzky?

7 Name the three brothers from Petrolia, Ontario, who combined to score 669 NHL goals in their careers.

8 Who was the last member of the Boston Bruins to score at least 50 goals in a single NHL regular season?

9 From 1968 until 1975, Bobby Orr of the Boston Bruins won the James Norris Trophy a record eight consecutive times as the NHL's outstanding defenseman. Who ended Orr's dominance of the Norris Trophy, in 1976?

10 With which NHL team did Darryl Sittler play the final season of his Hall of Fame career?

11 Who was the first NHL goaltender to popularize the use of the mask as a standard piece of goalie equipment?

12 In the 1979-80 season, Wayne Gretzky of the Edmonton Oilers was declared ineligible for NHL rookie of the year honors, due to the fact that he had played the previous season as a professional, in the World Hockey Association. Name the player who won the Calder Trophy in Gretzky's first season in the NHL.

13 Who was the first American-born player to be selected first overall in the NHL Entry Draft?

14 Name the members of the famed Los Angeles Kings forward line known as the "Triple Crown Line".

15 Who was the first member of the Toronto Maple Leafs to record at least 100 points in a single NHL season?

16 Who succeeded the retired Maurice Richard as captain of the Montreal Canadiens, for the 1960-61 NHL season?

QUIZ 17

1 Name the only three coaches in NHL history to have 500 or more NHL victories with one team.

2 On December 6th, 1995, the Colorado Avalanche dealt Andrei Kovalenko, Martin Rucinsky and Jocelyn Thibault to the Montreal Canadiens. Name the two player that the Avalanche received in this blockbuster trade.

3 Name the NHL goalkeeper who was known as "Hatchet Man".

4 The NHL record for shots on goal by a player in a single season stands at 550. Who holds this record?

5 Who was the first player in the National Hockey League to win the scoring title in consecutive seasons?

6 Name the only member of the Calgary Flames to have sweater number retired by the club.

7 Name the only member of the New York Islanders to win the Hart Memorial Trophy as the NHL's most valuable player.

8 Name the goaltender who holds the NHL record for the most victories in a single regular season.

9 Name the only two players in NHL history to score at least 50 goals in a season while still teenagers.

10 In 1963, the National Hockey League created the Amateur Draft as a means of phasing out the sponsorship of amateur teams by league member clubs. Who was the first player drafted in the 1963 Amateur Draft?

11 Who is the only player in NHL history to hold the franchise record for goals in a single season for two NHL teams?

12 Best known as member of the Montreal Canadiens, for which NHL franchise did Guy Lafleur play the final game of his illustrious career?

13 The National Hockey League expanded from 22 to 24 teams in 1992. Name the teams that were granted franchises to begin the 1992-93 season?

14 Name the Hockey Hall of Fame member who was known as the "Pembroke Peach".

15 Who was the first European-trained goaltender to win the Vezina Trophy as the NHL's top netminder?

16 Who was the first National Hockey League team to win the Stanley Cup, three years in succession?

1 Who is the only player in NHL history to record at least 200 points in a single regular season?

2 John Bucyk, Bronco Horvath and Vic Stasiuk of the Boston Bruins formed a high scoring forward line during the 1950s. What was the nickname of this fabulous Bruin line?

3 Name the only member of the Buffalo Sabres to score 5 goals in a single NHL game.

4 Who was the first rookie in NHL history to record at least 100 points in a single regular season?

5 Name the three goaltenders named to Team Canada for the 1972 Summit Series against Russia.

6 Who was the last member of the Edmonton Oilers to win the Hart Memorial Trophy as the NHL's most valuable player?

7 Wayne Gretzky's younger brother Brent played a total of 13 games in his National Hockey League career. For which team did Brent suit up for all 13?

8 Name the only member of the Chicago Blackhawks to win the James Norris Trophy as the NHL's top defenseman three consecutive times.

9 Who holds the Toronto Maple Leafs record for the most points in a single NHL season?

10 Who recorded the most playoff points in the history of the World Hockey Association?

11 With which franchise did Brendan Shanahan begin his NHL career?

12 Name the only three goaltenders in NHL history to win the Calder Memorial Trophy as the league's rookie of the year and the Vezina Trophy as the NHL's outstanding netminder, in the same year.

13 Name the four players to have their jersey numbers retired by the Los Angeles Kings.

14 Which NHL Original Six franchise currently suffers the longest drought between Stanley Cup Championships?

15 Who is the only team in NHL history to come back from a 3 games to none deficit in the Stanley Cup Finals, to win the Stanley Cup?

16 Name the only player in NHL history to score at least one goal in ten consecutive Stanley Cup Playoff games.

QUIZ 19

1 In 2005-06, Jaromir Jagr of the New York Rangers won the Art Ross Trophy as the National Hockey League's leading scorer. Who was the last member of an original six team to win the Art Ross Trophy, as the NHL's leading scorer?

2 Which NHL pugilist has been given the nickname "The Albanian Assassin"?

3 Who was the first goaltender to win the Conn Smythe Memorial Trophy as the NHL's most valuable player in the Stanley Cup Playoffs?

4 Who was the last President of the National Hockey League?

5 Name the NHL franchise that finished atop the NHL regular season standings a record setting seven times in succession.

6 Who was the last member of the Chicago Blackhawks to record at least 100 points in a single regular season?

7 The record for the fastest two goals by one player in a Stanley Cup Playoff game stands at 5 seconds. Who holds this seemingly unbreakable record?

8 Name the only defenseman in NHL history to have his sweater number retired by two different teams.

9 On March 13th, 1955, an incident took place at the Boston Garden that led to the infamous "Richard Riot" at the Montreal Forum four days later. Maurice Richard was suspended from the NHL for the remainder of the season (including the playoffs) for his attack on this Bruin defenseman. Name him.

10 For which Ontario Hockey Association franchise did both Bobby Hull and Stan Mikita play their major junior hockey?

11 What was the nickname given to Philadelphia Flyers enforcer Dave Schultz?

12 On December 19th, 1995, the Calgary Flames traded Joe Nieuwendyk to the Dallas Stars. Name the two players that the Flames acquired in this trade with Dallas.

13 Who was the first defenseman in NHL history to record a hat trick in a Stanley Cup Playoff game?

14 In the 1940s, the Chicago Blackhawks boasted an outstanding forward line known as the "Pony Line". Name the members of this top scoring trio of Blackhawks.

15 First awarded in 1948, the Art Ross Memorial Trophy was awarded to the National Hockey League's leading scorer during the regular season. Who was the inaugural winner of the Art Ross Trophy in 1948?

16 Who is the oldest player in NHL history to record at least 100 points in a single season?

1 Who was the last player to win the Lady Byng Memorial Trophy as the NHL's most gentlemanly player, in back to back seasons?

2 Who is known as the "Russian Rocket"?

3 Name the only three coaches in NHL history to lead their team to the Stanley Cup title five or more times.

4 Who holds the Detroit Red Wings franchise record for the most goals in a single NHL season?

5 Name the two players who share the NHL record for the most goals in a single Stanley Cup Playoff campaign.

6 Who is the only player in NHL history to average over two assists per game for one full NHL regular season?

7 Who is the only member of the Ottawa Senators to win the Calder Memorial Trophy as the NHL's rookie of the year?

8 Name the first coach of the Nashville Predators.

9 Who was the first defenseman in NHL history to score at least 20 goals in a single regular season?

10 In what year did the National Hockey League make the wearing of helmets mandatory for players entering the NHL?

11 Who was the last player to score five goals in a single Stanley Cup Playoff game?

12 Punch Imlach, coach and general manager of the Toronto Maple Leafs, once said of this Hall of Fame member, "Hockey is a streetcar named desire and he doesn't always catch it". To whom was Imlach referring?

13 Who is the only player in NHL history to win both the Hart Memorial Trophy as the NHL's most valuable player and the Frank J. Selke Trophy as the NHL's outstanding defensive forward, in the same season?

14 Name the only two forwards in NHL history to be selected to the First All-Star Team ten or more times in their careers.

15 Name the only goaltender in the history of the National Hockey League to appear in over 1000 regular season games in his career.

16 A player scoring four goals in a single NHL game is a relatively rare occurrence. Name the two members of the Ottawa Senators who both scored four times in the same game, in 2005.

QUIZ 21

1 Whose deadly accurate shot earned him the nickname "Old Poison"?

2 Name the only three players in NHL history to record over 100 assists in a single regular season.

3 During the 1960s, the Chicago Blackhawks featured a fabulous forward line known as "The Scooter Line". Name the members of this dynamic Hawk line.

4 Name the first Soviet-trained player to defect to North America to join a National Hockey League team?

5 Who was the first member of the New York Islanders to score at least 50 goals in a single NHL season?

6 On January 20th, 1982, the Toronto Maple Leafs sent disgruntled Darryl Sittler to the Philadelphia Flyers. Who did the Leafs receive in return for Sittler?

7 Who holds the National Hockey League record for the most 30 or more goal seasons in a career?

8 Who is the only Swedish-born player to win the Hart Memorial Trophy as the NHL's most valuable player?

9 Who has appeared in the most regular season games as a member of the Toronto Maple Leafs?

10 For what Western Hockey League team did sniper Jarome Iginla play his major junior hockey?

11 Who served as President of the National Hockey League from 1917, the time of the league's formation, until 1943, the dawn of hockey's modern era?

12 Name the only two players in NHL history to win the Hart Memorial Trophy as the NHL's most valuable player with two different teams.

13 Who was the first player in NHL history to play in 900 consecutive regular season games?

14 The NHL record for the fewest points by a team in a single regular season (minimum 70 game schedule) stands at 21. What team holds this dubious record?

15 Who was the last goaltender to be named the most valuable player in the NHL All-Star game?

16 Who was the coach of the Boston Bruins the last time they captured the Stanley Cup?

QUIZ 22

1 Name the only defenseman in NHL history to register six assists in a single game, in his rookie year.

2 Who holds the Buffalo Sabres franchise record for the most points in a single NHL game?

3 Elected posthumously to the Hockey Hall of Fame in 1971, his admission to the Hall caused Conn Smythe to resign his position on the Hall of Fame selection committee. Whose induction into the Hall of Fame prompted Smythe to make this rather drastic decision?

4 Who was the last member of the Toronto Maple Leafs to lead the National Hockey League in scoring?

5 Name the only three players in NHL history to win the Hart Memorial Trophy as the league's most valuable player during the regular season and the Conn Smythe Memorial Trophy as the NHL's most valuable player in the Stanley Cup Playoffs, in the same season.

6 Who was the first defenseman in NHL history to record a hat trick (3 goals in one game) in a Stanley Cup Finals game?

7 Who was the first European-trained player to score at least 50 goals in a single NHL season?

8 Who is the oldest player in NHL history to be selected as the winner of the Calder Memorial Trophy as the NHL's rookie of the year?

9 One of the most energetic and agitating players of all time, this terrific skater could also play with the best, as he proved throughout his NHL career. Who was fittingly nicknamed 'The Entertainer'?

10 Who was the last defenseman to record at least 100 points in a single NHL season?

11 Name the American University that both Ken Dryden and Joe Nieuwendyk played their NCAA hockey prior to making their NHL debut.

12 Who holds the World Hockey Association's record for the most points in a single regular season game?

13 The National Hockey League expanded from 16 to 18 teams to begin the 1974-75 schedule. Name the two teams that were added to the league.

14 Who is the only member of the Toronto Maple Leafs to win the Frank J. Selke Trophy as the NHL's outstanding defensive forward?

15 Who holds the NHL record for the most career shorthanded goals in the Stanley Cup Playoffs?

16 Who holds the single season record for the most points for a defenceman for both the Los Angeles Kings and the Washington Capitals?

1 Name the first round draft pick of the Toronto Maple Leafs who was given the nickname "Wild Thing".

2 Who was the first member of the Montreal Canadiens to record at least 100 points in a single regular season?

3 The Atlanta Thrashers were granted a National Hockey League franchise to begin the 1999-2000 season. Who did the Thrashers choose with their first pick of the 1999 NHL Entry Draft?

4 Who coached the Los Angeles Kings in their inaugural season in the National Hockey League?

5 During the depression years, the New York Rangers featured the forward line of Frank Boucher, Bill Cook and Bun Cook. What was this marvelous line's nickname?

6 Name the only player in NHL history to score all five of his team's goals in a Stanley Cup Playoff game.

7 Who has played in the most NHL All-Star games?

8 On March 11th, 2000, Bryan Berard of the Toronto Maple Leafs lost most of his sight in his right eye as a result of an accidental high stick. Whose stick struck Berard?

9 On May 10th, 1970, Bobby Orr of the Boston Bruins scored one of the most famous goals in Stanley Cup Playoff history. Who set up Orr's historic goal and who did he score it on?

10 Who was the first NHL goaltending tandem to share the Vezina Trophy?

11 Who was the first player in NHL history to win a major individual award despite the fact that he was traded during the season?

12 Who was the last member of the Montreal Canadiens to win the James Norris Trophy as the NHL's best defenseman?

13 Name the former member of the Toronto Maple Leafs who was given the nickname "The Milkman".

14 Who is the only player in NHL history to lead the league in goalscoring six consecutive times?

15 The record for goals scored by a player in a single NHL All-Star game stands at four. Name the five players who share this record.

16 Who was the first member of the NHL's Winnipeg Jets to score at least 50 goals in a single regular season?

QUIZ 24

1 On June 30th, 1992, the Quebec Nordiques traded a disgruntled Eric Lindros to the Philadelphia Flyers. Who did the Nordiques acquire to complete the deal for Lindros?

2 Who was the first defenseman to win the Calder Memorial Trophy as the NHL's rookie of the year?

3 Name the netminder who won an incredible 201 more games than he lost during his NHL career.

4 On December 4th, 1987, the Boston Bruins retired the number 7 of the great Phil Esposito. Who wore the number 7 prior to it being raised to the rafters of Boston Garden to honor Esposito?

5 Who was the first player in NHL history to score a goal on a penalty shot?

6 Name the only major NHL individual award that the legendary Maurice "Rocket" Richard won during his illustrious career.

7 For which Ontario Hockey League team did defensive specialist Bob Gainey play his major junior hockey?

8 Who finished second in voting for the Lady Byng Memorial Trophy as the NHL's most gentlemanly player a record-tying four years in succession, yet never did win the coveted award?

9 Name the record setting forward who is known as "The Finnish Flash".

10 Who succeeded George Armstrong as the captain of the Toronto Maple Leafs upon Armstrong's retirement at the end of the 1970-71 season?

11 What is the name of the Award presented to the most valuable player in United States College hockey?

12 For which Ontario Hockey Association team did the incomparable Bobby Orr play his major junior hockey?

13 Name the only two Russian-trained players to be selected first overall in the NHL Entry Draft.

14 Who holds the National Hockey League record for the most power play goals in a single season?

15 Who was the first member of the Calgary Flames to score at least 50 goals in a single season?

16 Name the only three players in NHL history to win the James Norris Trophy as the NHL's top defenseman at least five times during their careers.

QUIZ 25

1 Name the last NHL team to win the Stanley Cup in consecutive seasons.

2 Whose record did goalkeeper Patrick Roy surpass when he recorded his 448th NHL regular season victory?

3 Who was the last member of the Edmonton Oilers to record at least 100 points in a NHL season?

4 Harold Ballard, owner of the Toronto Maple Leafs said of this former player, "He could go into the corner with six eggs in his pocket and come out without any broken." To whom was Ballard referring?

5 With which World Hockey Association franchise did Wayne Gretzky begin his professional hockey career?

6 Who is the oldest player to win the Conn Smythe Memorial Trophy as the NHL's most valuable player in the Stanley Cup Playoffs?

7 Name the only member of the Chicago Blackhawks to score at least five goals in a single NHL game.

8 Name the 1940s Toronto Maple Leafs defense duo who were known as "The Gold Dust Twins".

9 Who was the first player in NHL history to win the Hart Memorial Trophy as the NHL's most valuable player in consecutive seasons?

10 What was the name of the first Philadelphia franchise to play in the National Hockey League?

11 Who holds the NHL record for the most points by a rookie defenseman in one season?

12 Wayne Gretzky holds the NHL record for scoring 50 goals in a season in the fewest number of games. How many games did it take "The Great One" to score 50 times, in establishing this record?

13 Name the only two members of the New Jersey Devils to win the Calder Memorial Trophy as the NHL's rookie of the year.

14 What was the name of the World Hockey Association's Calgary franchise that played in the league from 1975 until 1977?

15 Who was the last defenseman to win both the Hart Memorial Trophy as the NHL's MVP and the James Norris Trophy as the NHL's top defenseman in the same year?

16 The number 2 has been retired by three NHL teams. Name the players that have had their jersey number 2 retired.

QUIZ 26

1 On November 12th, 2005, the Montreal Canadiens retired the sweater number 12. Name the two players that the Canadiens honored by raising the number 12 to the rafters of the Bell Centre.

2 Name the Hall of Fame goaltender who was given the nickname "Mr. Zero".

3 For which Ontario Hockey League franchise did Joe Thornton play his major junior hockey?

4 Who is the only player in NHL history to win the Conn Smythe Trophy as the most valuable player in the Stanley Cup Playoffs three times in his career?

5 Who was the first player to score more than 50 goals in a NHL regular season?

6 Name the two players who share the NHL record for the most 50 or more goal seasons.

7 Name the only twin brothers to be selected in the first round of the NHL Entry Draft, by the same team.

8 Name the only goaltender in history to play in the National Hockey League in four different decades.

9 In what season did the National Hockey League introduce a five minute sudden-death overtime in regular season games that are tied at the end of regulation time?

10 Name the three brothers from Kirkland Lake, Ontario, who played a combined 1521 games in the National Hockey League.

11 Who is the only member of the New York Islanders to win the Art Ross Trophy as the NHL's leading point producer?

12 The Calder Trophy, first awarded in 1933, is presented to the player deemed to be the most proficient in his first year in the National Hockey League. Name the first winner of this prestigious trophy.

13 Name the two teams that have faced each other the most times in the NHL's Stanley Cup Finals.

14 Who is the only player in NHL history to be awarded two penalty shots in a single game?

15 Who holds the National Hockey League record for the most consecutive games played?

16 Wayne Gretzky set the NHL record for assists in one regular season in 1985-86 with 163. This was the fifth time that Gretzky had broken his own single season assists record. Who held the record prior to Gretzky?

QUIZ 27

1 Who was the last player to win three major individual NHL awards in the same season?

2 Name the former Calder Trophy candidate who was arrested in August 1977, at Toronto's International Airport when authorities found 4.5 grams of cocaine hidden in his sock in his luggage.

3 Only once in NHL history has the Vezina Trophy been awarded to two goaltenders from different teams. Name the two netminders who shared the Vezina Trophy in 1974.

4 Who holds the St. Louis Blues individual record for the most points in franchise history?

5 Name the NHL city that hosted the NHL Entry Draft from 1963 until 1984 inclusive.

6 Name the members of the famous Soviet forward line that were known as the "KLM line".

7 On March 23rd, 1952, Bill Mosienko of the Chicago Blackhawks scored 3 goals in just 21 seconds to establish the NHL record for the fastest 3 goals in a game by an individual. Who assisted on all 3 of Mosienko's markers?

8 Maurice Richard was known as "The Rocket". What nickname was bestowed on "The Rocket's" younger brother, Henri?

9 For which Quebec Major Junior Hockey League team did Mario Lemieux play his major junior hockey?

10 Who was the first player in NHL history to score on a penalty shot during a Stanley Cup Playoff game?

11 Name the only goaltender to be named captain of the Montreal Canadiens.

12 Who was known as 'Motor City Smitty'?

13 Who is the only man to have his name inscribed on the Stanley Cup as a player, coach and general manager?

14 In 1952-53, this future Hockey Hall of Fame member won the Calder Memorial Trophy as the NHL's rookie of the year. The following season he lost his job to another future Hall of Famer and did not appear in a single NHL game. Who were the goaltenders involved in this rather bizarre occurrence?

15 Who holds the National Hockey League record for the most points by an individual in a single game?

16 Name the team that holds the NHL record for the most losses in a single regular season.

QUIZ 28

1 Who was the first player in NHL history to record at least 20 points in a single Stanley Cup Playoff campaign?

2 Who was the first Swedish-born player to score at least fifty goals in a single NHL season?

3 Name the only man to play at least 1000 National Hockey League games as a member of the New Jersey Devils.

4 Who was the first player in National Hockey League history to score 500 goals in his career?

5 Wayne Gretzky recorded 7 assists in an NHL game an amazing 3 times during his career. Name the only other player in NHL history to manage 7 assists in a single game.

6 Who was the first member of the Toronto Maple Leafs to win the Vezina Trophy as the NHL's top goaltender?

7 With which Ontario Hockey League team did Eric Staal play his major junior hockey?

8 Who was the youngest defenseman in NHL history to score at least 30 goals in a single regular season?

9 Who is the only member of the Dallas Stars to win the Conn Smythe Memorial Trophy as the most valuable player in the Stanley Cup Playoffs?

10 The National Hockey League expanded from 28 to 30 teams to begin the 2000-01 season. Name the two cities that were granted NHL franchises in 2000.

11 Name the only defenseman in NHL history to win both the Calder Memorial Trophy as the NHL's rookie of the year and the Hart Memorial Trophy as the league's most valuable player in his NHL career.

12 Wayne Gretzky scored at least 70 goals in a season four times in his glorious career. Name the only other player in NHL history to score at least 70 times in three different seasons.

13 How many times have the Boston Bruins captured the Stanley Cup?

14 Who was the first coach of the Tampa Bay Lightning?

15 Who were the first brothers to be selected to the NHL's First All-Star Team in the same season?

16 Who was the last player to win the Hart Memorial Trophy as the NHL's most valuable player in back to back seasons?

QUIZ 29

1 In both 1995 and 1996, the Ottawa Senators had the first overall selection in the NHL Entry Draft. Who did the Senators select first overall in each of these Drafts?

2 Who is the only goaltender in National Hockey League history to record more than 100 regular season shutouts in his career?

3 Name the only two players in history to play at least 25 seasons in the National Hockey League.

4 Which National Hockey League team was notoriously nicknamed "The Broad Street Bullies"?

5 Who is the only man in NHL history to be inducted into the Hockey Hall of Fame immediately following his final game in the league?

6 Which NHL coach once said "Last season we couldn't win at home and we were losing on the road. My failure was that I couldn't think of any place else to play"?

7 Name the three brothers from Kirkland Lake, Ontario, who all played defense for the St. Louis Blues from 1968 until 1972.

8 Who is the only player to score at least 500 regular season NHL goals as a member of the New York Islanders?

9 Who was the last player to score 4 goals in the NHL All-Star game?

10 Who was the first player in NHL history to score 50 goals in a season playing for two different teams?

11 What former first overall selection in the National Hockey League Entry Draft goes by the nickname "The Big E"?

12 The Buffalo Sabres retired the number 18 of Danny Gare and the number 16 of Pat Lafontaine during the 2005-06 NHL season. Name the four other players that have had their jerseys retired by the Sabres.

13 Who holds the single season NHL record for the most goals by a defenseman in the Stanley Cup Playoffs?

14 Mike Gartner scored 708 goals in his NHL career. Name the five teams that Gartner played for during his productive career.

15 Name the only coach in NHL history to win over 200 Stanley Cup Playoff games.

16 On June 28th, 1994, a blockbuster trade took place between the Toronto Maple Leafs and the Quebec Nordiques. The Leafs acquired Mats Sundin, Garth Butcher and Todd Warriner in the deal. Who did the Nordiques receive in return?

QUIZ 30

1 Who was the first member of the Detroit Red Wings to score at least 50 goals in a single NHL season?

2 Name the former winner of the Calder Memorial Trophy who went by the nickname "Turk".

3 Clarence Campbell served as President of the National Hockey League from 1946 until his retirement in 1977. Who succeeded Campbell as NHL President?

4 Who was the last player to score at least 50 goals, to average over a goal a game in a single NHL regular season?

5 With which Ontario Hockey Leauge team did Jonathan Cheecho play his major junior hockey?

6 Maurice "Rocket" Richard was the first player in NHL history to score 50 goals in a single season. Who was next to accomplish this feat?

7 Who was the first coach of the Florida Panthers?

8 Who is the only member of the Toronto Maple Leafs to capture the Lady Byng Trophy as the NHL's most gentlemanly player in consecutive seasons?

9 Name the only two men to play 1000 or more NHL games as members of the Buffalo Sabres.

10 Who was the last member of the Calgary Flames to record at least 100 points in a single NHL regular season?

11 Name the three players who were members of both Team Canada 1972 and Team Canada 1974 that faced off against the Russians.

12 Who is the only player in NHL history to be awarded two penalty shots in one Stanley Cup Playoff campaign?

13 Name the only father and son tandem to have their names inscribed on the Hart Memorial Trophy as the National Hockey League's most valuable player?

14 Who is the only man in NHL history to coach in over 2000 regular season games?

15 Who was the last member of the New York Rangers to win the Lady Byng Trophy as the NHL's most gentlemanly player?

16 Who was the first player in NHL history to record at least 50 points in a single regular season?

1 Who holds the National Hockey League record for the longest winning streak by a goaltender in a single season?

2 The 1971 National Hockey League Entry Draft must be considered one of the best of all time. Who were the first two players selected in the 1971 Entry Draft?

3 Name the only player to score at least 500 career goals as a member of the Boston Bruins.

4 Name the NHL "tough guy" who was bestowed with the nickname "Bugsy".

5 Name the four players who managed to score at least 50 goals in their rookie year in the league.

6 Name the three Detroit Red Wing goaltenders who have won the Calder Memorial Trophy as the NHL's rookie of the year.

7 Who was the first European-trained NHLer to be inducted into the Hockey Hall of Fame?

8 Who was the last member of the Chicago Blackhawks to be named to the National Hockey League's First All-Star Team?

9 Who set an NHL record when he scored his first NHL goal at the 15 second mark of the first period of his first NHL game?

10 Name the goaltender who became the first big name to jump from the National Hockey League to the rival World Hockey Association when he signed with the Philadelphia Blazers in April of 1972.

11 Who is the only member of the Washington Capitals to win the James Norris Trophy as the NHL's best defenseman?

12 In 1946, Gordie Howe began his NHL career as a member of the Detroit Red Wings. Who won the Calder Memorial Trophy as the NHL's rookie of the year in Howe's rookie season?

13 The NHL record for the most points by an individual in a Stanley Cup Playoff game stands at eight. Name the two players who share this record.

14 Name the arena in which the Boston Bruins played their National Hockey League home games from 1924 until 1996.

15 Name the three players who scored over 500 goals as members of the Montreal Canadiens.

16 What Hockey Hall of Fame member was given the nickname "Old Boot Nose"?

1 What nation did the United States defeat in the final game of the 1980 Winter Olympics to secure the gold medal in hockey?

2 Name the only two members of the Toronto Maple Leafs to win the Hart Memorial Trophy as the NHL's most valuable player.

3 Name the Canadian author who penned the children's classics 'Boy on Defense', 'Scrubs on Skates' and 'The Leafs I Knew'.

4 Who led the National Hockey League in scoring five times during the 1950s?

5 Who is the only player in NHL history to record four hat tricks in one Stanley Cup Playoff year?

6 Possessing incredible first jump speed this member of the Hockey Hall of Fame was known as "The Roadrunner". Name him.

7 The incomparable Bobby Orr wore jersey number 4 throughout his glorious NHL career. However, in his first NHL All-Star game in 1968 he donned number 5. Why?

8 What was the name of the series of games between the Soviet Union and Team NHL that replaced the 1979 NHL All-Star game?

9 Who is the only player to record over 1000 career NHL points as a member of the New York Rangers?

10 Name the only team in the history of the National Hockey League to score 400 or more goals in a single season.

11 Name the NHL all-time great who was nicknamed "The Big Bomber".

12 Who was the youngest player to participate in a game in the history of the National Hockey League?

13 Who holds the NHL record for the most goals scored by a defenseman in a single season?

14 Who is the only member of the Pittsburgh Penguins to win the Frank J. Selke Trophy as the NHL's outstanding defensive forward?

15 Name the only member of the Tampa Bay Lightning to win the Hart Memorial Trophy as the NHL's most valuable player.

16 Best known as a member of the Montreal Canadiens, Larry Robinson played his final 3 NHL seasons with which team?

1 Who is the only player to record over 2000 minutes in penalties as a member of the Vancouver Canucks?

2 Who was the first United States born player to score 500 goals in his National Hockey League career?

3 King Clancy said of this hockey legend: "He could start on a dime and hit full speed within a couple of strides and he had about the strongest legs I've ever seen on a hockey player". To whom was Clancy referring?

4 The Washington Capitals franchise record for goals scored by an individual in a singe season stands at 60. Who holds this record?

5 Who was the last player to win the Hart Memorial Trophy as the NHL's most valuable player, despite the fact that his team missed the Stanley Cup Playoffs that season?

6 Name the only two defensemen in NHL history to be selected first overall in the NHL Entry Draft who have gone on to capture the Calder Memorial Trophy as the NHL's rookie of the year.

7 Who was the last member of the Detroit Red Wings to win the Lady Byng Trophy as the NHL's most gentlemanly player?

8 Name the four players in history who have managed to score 500 NHL goals in fewer than 700 NHL games.

9 Who was the first coach of the Columbus Blue Jackets?

10 Name the only two players to score more than 500 NHL goals as members of the Chicago Blackhawks.

11 The World Hockey Association was founded in January, 1971. Name the two men who are recognized as the founding fathers of the WHA.

12 The Buffalo Sabres' fabulous "French Connection" was perhaps the most dominant forward unit in the National Hockey League during the 1970s. Name the three members of the "French Connection".

13 Who was the first player in NHL history to score two shorthanded goals in a single Stanley Cup Playoff game?

14 Who is the only member of the Los Angeles Kings to win the James Norris Trophy as the NHL's top defenseman?

15 Who is the youngest goaltender to appear in an NHL All-Star game?

16 Known for his competitive spirit, this tenacious centerman was given the nickname "Killer". Name him.

QUIZ 34

1 Gordie Howe's brother Vic played a total of 33 games in his NHL career. For which team did Vic play all 33?

2 Only three teams have won the Stanley Cup as many as four times in succession. Name the teams that have achieved this feat.

3 Name the netminder who recorded the most career shutouts in the short history of the World Hockey Association.

4 Who was the coach of the New York Rangers the last time that the Rangers captured the Stanley Cup?

5 Who was given the short-lived nickname "Brinks", near the beginning of his NHL career?

6 On August 7th, 1992, the Chicago Blackhawks acquired Stephane Beauregard and a fourth round draft pick from the Buffalo Sabres. Who did the Sabres receive in return?

7 Name the only player in history to appear in the NHL All-Star game in five different decades.

8 Name the three goaltenders who were named to Canada's 2002 Olympic hockey squad.

9 Who was the first player in NHL history to score at least 50 goals in a season for two different teams?

10 Who holds the National Hockey League record for the longest undefeated streak by a goaltender?

11 The first NHL All-Star game was played on February 14th, 1934, at the fabled Maple Leaf Gardens. The game was held as a benefit for which NHL veteran?

12 Who is the only player to play in over 1000 NHL games as a member of the Edmonton Oilers?

13 When Maurice "Rocket" Richard set an NHL record for goal scoring in a single season in 1944-45 he eclipsed the previous record of 44 goals in a season. Who held the record prior to Richard?

14 With which NHL team did Hockey Hall of Fame member Pat Lafontaine play the final game of his stellar career?

15 Who was the first player in NHL history to win the Calder Memorial Trophy as the league's rookie of the year, to go on to capture the Hart Memorial Trophy as the NHL's most valuable player later in his career?

16 Name the goalkeeper against whom Steve Yzerman, Joe Mullen and Brendan Shanahan all scored their 500th career NHL goal.

1 Who holds the New York Islander franchise record for the most points in a single NHL game?

2 What was the name of the Cincinnati franchise that were members of the World Hockey Association?

3 Name the only three players in NHL history to score at least 40 goals in a season 10 or more times during their careers.

4 Phil Esposito began his NHL career in 1963-64 playing 27 games for the Chicago Blackhawks that season. Who won the Calder Trophy in Esposito's rookie NHL season?

5 The NHL franchise in Toronto became known as the Maple Leafs partway through the 1926-27 season. What was the name of the Toronto team prior to being renamed the Maple Leafs?

6 Who coached the Edmonton Oilers to their four Stanley Cup Championships in the 1980s?

7 Name the defenseman who finished runner-up in voting for the Norris Trophy as the NHL's outstanding defenseman a record tying six times during his career, yet never did win this illustrious trophy.

8 Name the Philadelphia Flyer pugilist who was given the nickname "Battleship"?

9 Who was the last member of the Toronto Maple Leafs to lead the NHL in scoring during the Stanley Cup Playoffs?

10 Since 1967, there have been only two all-Canadian Stanley Cup Finals. Name the Canadian-based teams that were involved in both of these Finals?

11 Soviet coach Victor Tikhonov called this left winger "the best player in the world from a technical point of view". Of whom was Tikhonov referring?

12 Name the only three defensemen in NHL history to record over 30 points in one Stanley Cup Playoff year.

13 Name the broadcaster who made the phrase "He shoots, he scores" famous.

14 Who was the first player in NHL history to score 40 goals or more in his rookie season?

15 Perhaps the finest forward line in all of hockey during the 1970s belonged to the Winnipeg Jets of the World Hockey Association. Name this talented trio, who led the Jets to WHA supremacy in the 1970s.

16 Who was the first player in NHL history to play in at least 900 consecutive NHL regular season games?

QUIZ 36

1 The International tournament known as the Canada Cup was first held in 1976. Name the six nations that were invited to participate in the inaugural Canada Cup?

2 Who has recorded the most three or more goal games in the history of the National Hockey League?

3 Name the only coach in NHL history to win consecutive Stanley Cup titles with two different teams.

4 Who holds the National Hockey League single season record for the most assists by a goaltender?

5 On June 6th, 1972, the National Hockey League expanded from 14 to 16 teams. Name the two teams that were granted entry to the NHL to begin the 1972-73 season.

6 Name the NHL and WHA veteran whose tremendous size, strength and skating ability earned him the nickname "Swoop".

7 Who is the only position player (non-goaltender) to win the Calder Memorial Trophy as the NHL's rookie of the year and earn a berth on the NHL's First All-Star Team as a rookie?

8 Who is the only goalkeeper in National Hockey League history to win the Vezina Trophy five consecutive times?

9 Name the only player to participate in over 1000 NHL games as a member of the Philadelphia Flyers?

10 For which Quebec Major Junior Hockey League team did goaltender Patrick Roy play his major junior hockey?

11 How many times has Great Britain captured the Olympic Gold Medal in hockey?

12 When Bobby Hull of the Chicago Blackhawks scored a then record 58 goals during the 1968-69 season, he eclipsed the record of 54 goals that he had set in the 1965-66 season. Name the three players who shared the NHL record of 50 goals in a season prior to Hull's 54?

13 Name the three player who shared the Maurice "Rocket" Richard Trophy as the NHL's leading goal scorer in 2003-04.

14 Who was the first member of the Mighty Ducks of Anaheim to score at least 50 goals in a single NHL season?

15 Who was the first player in NHL history to participate in at least 100 Stanley Cup Playoff games?

16 The record for the longest winning streak by a team in one NHL season stands at 17 games. Which team set this remarkable record?

1 Name the 1970s Philadelphia Flyer star who was nicknamed "The Riverton Rifle"?

2 Who was the last member of the Montreal Canadiens to record at least 100 points in a single NHL season?

3 From 1955 until 1962, Doug Harvey captured the James Norris Trophy as the NHL's outstanding defenseman seven times in eight years. Who won the Norris Trophy in 1959, to interrupt Harvey's dominance of the award?

4 Who was the last member of the New York Rangers to win the Calder Memorial Trophy as the NHL's rookie of the year?

5 Who was the last player to remain active in the National Hockey League, who began his professional career as a member of the World Hockey Association?

6 Name the two goaltending brothers who were the first to face each other in a National Hockey League game.

7 Who said "I skate to where the puck is going to be, not to where it has been"?

8 Name the three members of the Montreal Canadiens "Sizzle Line".

9 Who was the first player in National Hockey League history to score at least 100 points in a season for two different teams?

10 Name the only two coaches to coach over 1000 National Hockey League games with one team.

11 Name the goaltender who holds the National Hockey League record for the most shutouts in one Stanley Cup Playoff year.

12 What was the name of the San Diego entry in the World Hockey Association?

13 Since 1967, only two players have managed to score 6 goals in a single National Hockey League game. Name them.

14 Who was the first netminder to win the Hart Memorial Trophy as the NHL's most valuable player?

15 For which National Hockey League team did Frank Mahovlich record the 500th goal of his outstanding career?

16 Name the player who holds the NHL record for the most consecutive years appearing in the Stanley Cup Playoffs.

QUIZ 38

1 Name the rugged and frenetic winger who went by the nickname "Spinner"?

2 With which National Hockey League team did the legendary Bobby Orr play the final game of his incomparable career?

3 Who was the last NHL goaltender to appear in every one of his team's games in a single regular season?

4 Name the only player in history to score four game winning goals in one Stanley Cup Playoff Series.

5 Name the last member of the Toronto Maple Leafs to be named to the National Hockey League's First All-Star team.

6 Which NHL team drafted Peter Forsberg in the first round of the 1991 NHL Entry Draft?

7 Who finished second in voting for the Hart Memorial Trophy as the NHL's most valuable player a record four times in his NHL career?

8 Who is the only member of the New Jersey Devils to win the Frank J. Selke Trophy as the NHL's best defensive forward?

9 Name the first team in National Hockey League history to have four players record at least 100 points in the same season.

10 Who won the Stanley Cup in 1927, the first year that the National Hockey League assumed control of the Stanley Cup competition?

11 Who holds the National Hockey League record for the most shorthanded goals by a defenseman in a single season?

12 Whom did Clarence Campbell succeed as President of the National Hockey League?

13 Name the arena in which the Buffalo Sabres played their NHL home games from 1970 until 1996.

14 The second edition of the international tournament known as the Canada Cup took place in 1981. Who was voted the most valuable player of this tournament?

15 The Boston Bruins of the 1930s and 1940s featured an outstanding forward line known as the "Kraut Line". Name the famed trio who formed the Bruins' "Kraut Line".

16 Name the NHL journeyman defenseman who went by the nickname "Radar".

1 How many times have the New Jersey Devils won the Stanley Cup?

2 The Philadelphia Flyers have had the first overall selection in the NHL Entry Draft only once in their history. Name the player that the Flyers chose with their only first overall pick.

3 Name the only four NHL players to score 100 or more goals in their Stanley Cup Playoff careers.

4 The NHL record for the most games played by a player in a single season stands at 86. Name the two players who share this record.

5 Who was the first player in National Hockey League history to score at least 10 shorthanded goals in a single regular season?

6 In 2000, the National Hockey League suspended Marty McSorley of the Boston Bruins for the final 23 games of the regular season and later extended the suspension to last exactly one year. Who did McSorley attack, prompting the NHL to issue the longest suspension in league history?

7 Who was the all time leading point producer in the history of the World Hockey Association?

8 Name the three players who have recorded over 1000 NHL points as members of the Chicago Blackhawks.

9   Who was the coach of the Montreal Canadiens the last time that the Habitants captured the Stanley Cup?

10   Who was know as "Tony O"?

11   Name the only team in National Hockey League history to be down three games to none in the Stanley Cup Final, and come back and win four straight games to capture the Cup.

12   Name the only three players in NHL history to be penalized over 400 minutes in a single season?

13   Name the Hockey Hall of Fame member who was nicknamed "The Old Lamplighter"?

14   Wayne Gretzky won the Hart Memorial Trophy as the NHL's most valuable player eight times in succession from 1980 until 1987. Who ended Gretzky's incredible winning streak in 1988?

15   How many times has Canada captured the Olympic Gold Medal in hockey?

16   Who is the only member of the Philadelphia Flyers to lead the National Hockey League in goal scoring in a single regular season?

1 The Pittsburgh Penguins chose Jaromir Jagr with the fifth overall selection of the 1990 NHL Entry Draft. Who was taken first overall in the 1990 Entry Draft?

2 Who set the National Hockey League single season scoring record when he recorded 96 points in the 1958-59 season, a record that would stand for seven seasons?

3 Name the three current National Hockey League teams that have won the Stanley Cup only once during their franchise history.

4 Name the Philadelphia Flyer netminder who was killed in an alcohol-related traffic mishap in November of 1985.

5 Who is the only United States-born player to win the Conn Smythe Memorial Trophy as the most valuable player in the Stanley Cup Playoffs?

6 Who was the first player in NHL history to record over 100 points and 200 penalty minutes in the same season?

7 With which Wetern Hockey League team did Ryan Smith play his major junior hockey?

8 On July 27th, 1995, the Hartford Whalers traded defenseman Chris Pronger to the St. Louis Blues. Whom did the Whalers receive in return for Pronger?

9 Who has scored the most career points in the Stanley Cup Playoffs as a member of the Montreal Canadiens?

10 Name the only two players in National Hockey League history to score over 800 regular season goals in their NHL careers.

11 Who was the first coach of the New York Rangers?

12 The number 10 jersey has been retired by only three National Hockey League teams! Name the three players that have seen their number 10 jerseys raised to the rafters.

13 Who is the only US-born player in NHL history to score at least 50 goals in three consecutive seasons?

14 Who is the only player to score the 500th goal of his National Hockey League career while a member of the Washington Capitals?

15 Who is the only man to coach both the Montreal Canadiens and the Toronto Maple Leafs to Stanley Cup Championships?

16 Name the fearless and sometimes flaky NHL goaltender who said: "Anyone who wears one is chicken. My face is my mask".

QUIZ 41

1 Name the only defenseman in National Hockey League history to record two hat tricks (3-goal games) in the Stanley Cup Playoffs, during his career?

2 Name the only player to score over 400 NHL regular season goals as a member of the Philadelphia Flyers?

3 Name the NHL "Ironman" who went by the nickname "Fats".

4 Who are the only three players to be named the winner of the James Norris Trophy as the NHL's best defenseman with two different teams?

5 Who was the first member of the Toronto Maple Leafs to win Calder Memorial Trophy as the NHL's rookie of the year?

6 Name the two teams that participated in the only Stanley Cup Final that saw each and every game decided in overtime.

7 Who coached the Minnesota North Stars in their inaugural season in the National Hockey League?

8 Who was the last player to win the Lester B. Pearson Award as the NHL's most valuable, as voted by the NHLPA, in back to back seasons?

9 Who is the only member of the New York Islanders to win the Vezina Trophy as the NHL's top netminder?

10 During the 1988 Stanley Cup Playoffs this New Jersey Devils coach was suspended by the National Hockey League for his verbal attack on referee Don Koharski. Who uttered the infamous quote "have another donut, you fat pig!"?

11 The Ottawa Senators chose Jason Spezza of the OHL's Windsor Spitfires with the 2nd overall selection of the 2001 NHL Entry Draft. Who captured the Calder Memorial Trophy as the NHL's rookie of the year in 2001-02, Spezza's first season in the league?

12 Who is the longest-serving captain in the history of the Toronto Maple Leafs?

13 Name the only two members of the St. Louis Blues to win the James Norris Trophy as the national Hockey League's best defenseman.

14 Who was voted the most valuable player of the 1976 Canada Cup?

15 Name the only four players in NHL history who have accumulated at least 200 points in their Stanley Cup Playoff careers.

16 The record for the most losses suffered by a goaltender in a single NHL season stands at 48. Who holds this dubious record?

QUIZ 42

1 Name the only player in NHL history to play in the Stanley Cup Finals ten times and come away on the winning side in all ten.

2 Name the legendary goaltender who was given the nickname "St. Patrick".

3 With which Quebec Major Junior Hockey League team did Jeremy Roenick play his major junior hockey?

4 Who is the only player in NHL history to captain two different franchises to Stanley Cup Championships?

5 On August 23rd, 2005, the Ottawa Senators acquired forward Dany Heatley from the Atlanta Thrashers. Name the two players that the Senators sent to the Thrashers to complete the Heatley trade.

6 Name the players who have had their number 7 jersey retired by the Boston Bruins, Detroit Red Wings, New York Rangers and Montreal Canadiens?

7 Who scored at least one goal in 13 consecutive NHL games during the 1979-80 season, the longest scoring streak in the NHL since the 1920s?

8 Which classy NHL centerman is nicknamed "Stevie Wonder"?

9 Name the only goaltender to play for five of the Original Six National Hockey League teams.

10 Name the brothers who combined to score an incredible 1319 goals during their NHL careers.

11 How many times has the United States won the Olympic Gold Medal in hockey?

12 Who was the first member of the Buffalo Sabres to record at least 100 points in a single NHL regular season?

13 Name the only player in NHL history to win the Lady Byng Trophy as the NHL's most gentlemanly player and the Conn Smythe Memorial Trophy as the most valuable player in the Stanley Cup Playoffs, in the same season.

14 Who was the Toronto Maple Leafs' opponent in both the first NHL game played at Maple Leaf Gardens and the last NHL game played at the fabled arena?

15 Name the only three defensemen to play in over 1600 regular season National Hockey games.

16 Name the National Hockey League city that is often referred to as "Hockeytown".

QUIZ 43

1 Name the only player in NHL history to score all of his team's goals in a single game while scoring five times during the game.

2 Who is the only goaltender in NHL history to record two undefeated streaks of longer than 25 games?

3 Who did American sports writers dub "The Babe Ruth of Hockey"?

4 Who is the only player to score 500 NHL goals as a member of the Buffalo Sabres?

5 Rick Nash was chosen first overall by the Columbus Blue Jackets in the 2002 NHL Entry Draft. For which Ontario Hockey League team did Nash play his major junior hockey?

6 Name the goaltender who holds the National Hockey League record for the most shutouts in one Stanley Cup Playoff year.

7 What was the name of Minnesota's entry in the World Hockey Association?

8 Who is known by the rather unflattering nickname "Side Show Bob"?

9 Name the future Hall of Famer who was tragically killed in an automobile accident on February 21st, 1974.

10 Who holds the National Hockey League record for the most career game-winning goals?

11 Who is the only player in history to win the Lady Byng Memorial Trophy as the NHL's most gentlemanly player as both a forward and a defenseman?

12 Name the only goaltender in NHL history to win the Hart Memorial Trophy as the NHL's most valuable player even though his club finished in the basement of the NHL?

13 Name the only two members of the Montreal Canadiens to score as many as eight points in a single NHL game?

14 Name the three members of the St. Louis Blues to be selected as the most valuable player in the NHL All-Star game?

15 Who was named as the first coach of the NHL's Minnesota Wild?

16 Name the only two members of the Winnipeg Jets to win the Calder Memorial Trophy as the NHL's rookie of the year.

1 Bobby Orr held the NHL record for the most career points by a defenseman for more than five years. Who was the first defenseman to eclipse Orr's point total?

2 Who holds the NHL record for the most career shorthanded goals?

3 Name the first team in NHL history to have five players score at least 30 goals in the same season.

4 Who is the only player in NHL history to win the Conn Smythe Memorial Trophy as the most valuable player in the Stanley Cup Playoffs with two different teams?

5 Who was often referred to as the "Ultimate Bruin"?

6 Name the only two goaltenders to be selected first overall in the National Hockey League Entry Draft?

7 Who is the only player in National Hockey League history to score seven goals in a single game?

8 Who was the last member of the Montreal Canadiens to win the Calder Memorial Trophy as NHL's rookie of the year?

9 Name the members of the Chicago Blackhawks famed "Million Dollar Line".

10 On November 19th, 1998, a sucker punch delivered by Matt Johnson of the Los Angeles Kings, led to the retirement of this four-time Stanley Cup champion. Name him.

11 Name the team that holds the National Hockey League record of 38 consecutive road losses.

12 Bobby Hull began his NHL career with the Chicago Blackhawks in the 1957-58 season. Who won the Calder Memorial Trophy as the NHL's rookie of the year in Hull's first season in the league?

13 Name the only two players in NHL history to record a Plus/Minus of over plus 100 in a single season.

14 Wayne Gretzky recorded 150 or more points in a single NHL season nine times during his career while Mario Lemieux has scored at least 150 points in a season on four occasions. Name the three other NHLers to record at least 150 points in a single season.

15 Who was the first coach to win the Jack Adams Award as the National Hockey League's coach of the year with different teams?

16 What NHL team has won a record 19 consecutive Stanley Cup Playoff series?

QUIZ 45

1 Who holds the NHL record for the fastest four goals by an individual in a single game?

2 Name the Timmins, Ontario born brothers who were known as "The Big M" and "The Little M".

3 Who were the first brothers to be selected in the first round of the National Hockey League Entry Draft in the same year?

4 Until 1981 the Vezina Trophy was awarded to the goaltender(s) of the NHL team allowing the fewest goals against during the regular season. Name the first goaltending tandem to share the Vezina Trophy.

5 Who was the first player in NHL history to score the Stanley Cup winning goal in back to back seasons?

6 Name the only player in NHL history to score at least 30 power play goals in a season twice in his career.

7 Who is the last member of the Boston Bruins to win the Lady Byng Trophy as the NHL's most gentlemanly player?

8 Considered to be one the greatest pests in NHL history, this player was fittingly nicknamed "The Rat". Name him.

9   Name the only three players in history to play in over 1700 NHL games during their careers.

10   Who was known simply as "the Flower"?

11   Name the only team in NHL history to come back from a 3 games to one deficit in a Stanley Cup Playoff series, to win, twice in the same season.

12   Who was the first player of Afro-American descent to play a game in the National Hockey League?

13   What was the name of Toronto's entry in the World Hockey Association?

14   Who led the Russians in scoring during the classic 1972 Canada/Russia Summit Series?

15   Name the player who holds the National Hockey League record for the longest consecutive game point scoring streak by a defenseman.

16   Who is the only player in NHL history to be penalized over 700 minutes in his Stanley Cup Playoff career?

1 Who holds the single season NHL record for the most wins by a rookie goaltender?

2 Who was the first member of the New York Islanders to capture the Calder Memorial Trophy as the NHL's rookie of the year?

3 Name the only member of the Montreal Canadiens to score six goals in a single NHL game.

4 Who was the first member of the Vancouver Canucks to score at least 50 goals in a single NHL season?

5 For which team did Darryl Sittler record the 1000th point of his National Hockey League career?

6 Who are the only two members of the Detroit Red Wings to win the Lester B. Pearson Award as the most valuable player in the NHL as judged by the National Hockey League's Players Association?

7 Maurice "Rocket" Richard finished his career in 1960 with an NHL record 82 goals in the Stanley Cup Playoffs. Who was the first player to exceed Richard's playoff goal total?

8 Name the only two defensemen in National Hockey League history to appear in over 600 games with two different teams.

9 On June 30th, 2001, the Detroit Red Wings traded forward Vyacheslav Kozlov and a 2002 first round draft choice to the Buffalo Sabres. Who did the Red Wings receive in return?

10 Who is the only player in NHL history to score an even strength, power play, short-handed, penalty shot and empty net goal in the same game?

11 Name the only two players in history to win the Hart Memorial Trophy as the NHL's most valuable player at least five times during their careers.

12 The Mighty Ducks of Anaheim began play in the National Hockey League in 1993-94. Who was the first player that the Ducks selected in the 1993 NHL Entry Draft?

13 On January 12th, 2006, the New York Rangers retired the number 11 jersey of Mark Messier. Name the only other Rangers to be so honored.

14 Name the two members of the New Jersey Devils who each scored four goals in a game on October 28th, 2000, an achievement that had only been accomplished once before in NHL history.

15 Name the last nation to win the World Junior Hockey Championship in consecutive years.

16 Who is the only defenseman in NHL history to record more than 3000 minutes in penalties during his career?

1 Who holds the NHL record for the most game winning goals in a single Stanley Cup Playoff year?

2 To whom was Steve Shutt of the Montreal Canadiens referring when he said "Any guy who would be in his uniform, skates tied tight, sweater on and a stick beside him at 4 o'clock in the afternoon for an 8 o'clock game has to be strange"?

3 Name the National Hockey League goalkeeper who is known as "The Bullin Wall".

4 Who is the longest serving head coach in the history of the Buffalo Sabres franchise?

5 Who was the last goaltender to record three consecutive shutouts in the Stanley Cup Playoffs?

6 Name the only United States born player to be named to the National Hockey League's First All-Star Team at least five times.

7 With which Western Hockey League team did Calgary Flames' Dion Phaneuf play his major junior hockey?

8 The last time that an NHL team can boast having the Calder Memorial Trophy winner as the NHL's rookie of the year in consecutive seasons was 1967 and 1968. Name the players who took home the Calder and the team they won it with.

9 Name the siblings who between them have had their names inscribed on the Stanley Cup, as players, nineteen times.

10 Who was the first Russian-born player to be inducted into the Hockey Hall of Fame?

11 On June 13th, 1961, in a shocking trade, the Montreal Canadiens sent legendary defenseman Doug Harvey to the New York Rangers. Who did the Rangers give up to get Harvey?

12 In 1984-85, for the first time in history, two European-trained players were named to the National Hockey League's First All-Star Team. Name the two Europeans who were selected first team all-stars in 1984-85.

13 Name the Hockey Hall of Fame member who often referred to himself as "Old Blinky".

14 Who was the last member of the Toronto Maple Leafs to record at least 100 points in a single NHL regular season?

15 Name the only team in NHL history to have had three defenseman score at least 20 goals in the same season.

16 Who was the first European-trained player to record at least 100 points in a single NHL regular season?

QUIZ 48

1 The first time that the National Hockey League Entry Draft was held outside of Canada was in 1987. Name the American city that hosted the 1987 Draft.

2 Name the stalwart Chicago Blackhawk defenseman who went by the nickname "Moose".

3 What was the name of the Ottawa entry in the World Hockey Association?

4 Name the only two defensemen to win the Lady Byng Memorial Trophy as the NHL's most gentlemanly player.

5 Who was the last member of the Montreal Canadiens to be named to the NHL's First All-Star Team?

6 Name the two players who tied in voting for the Hart Memorial Trophy as the NHL's most valuable player in 2002.

7 With which team did Phil Housley play the final game of his NHL career?

8 Name the NHL goaltender who was often referred to as "Apple Cheeks".

9 Who was the first goaltender in National Hockey League history to be credited with scoring a goal?

10 Name the only two players in the glorious history of the Montreal Canadiens to play as many as twenty seasons for the team.

11 Who scored the tournament winning goal in the inaugural Canada Cup in 1976?

12 Who was once described by the *Boston Globe* as "Nureyev on ice"?

13 Name the only two members of the Philadelphia Flyers to win the Lester B. Pearson Award as the NHL's outstanding player as chosen by the National Hockey League's Players Association.

14 Who was the first player in National Hockey League history to score at least 20 goals in a season for six different teams?

15 On March 3rd, 1968 the Detroit Red Wings traded Paul Henderson, Norm Ullman and Floyd Smith to the Toronto Maple Leafs. Who did the Maple Leafs send to the Red Wings to complete the blockbuster trade?

16 Name the only player in NHL history to win the Frank J. Selke Trophy as the NHL's best defensive forward, with two different teams.

1 Who coached the Montreal Canadiens to a National Hockey League record, five consecutive Stanley Cup Championships?

2 Who is the only member of the Vancouver Canucks to have his jersey number retired?

3 Who was the last defenseman to be selected first overall in the National Hockey League Entry Draft to go on to win the Calder Memorial Trophy as the NHL's rookie of the year later in his career?

4 Who holds the National Hockey League record for the most power-play goals in a career?

5 When asked by a reporter what he had for his pre-game meal, he replied "a steak and a blonde". Name him.

6 Who was the first player to score three penalty shot goals in a single NHL season?

7 Name the expansion team and their coach that advanced to the Stanley Cup Finals in each of their first three seasons in the National Hockey League.

8 What team holds the National Hockey League record of 20 consecutive home ice victories in a single season?

9 Name the only two players in National Hockey league history to play at least 24 seasons for one NHL team.

10 Name the only five players to appear in over 1000 NHL games as members of the Toronto Maple Leafs.

11 Name the player who holds the National Hockey League record for the most goals scored during a single regular season.

12 Who is the only player in history to score over 500 career goals yet not record 1000 points during his NHL career?

13 Name the Hockey Hall of Fame coach who was dubbed "Captain Video".

14 Who was the last member of the Toronto Maple Leafs to be named the most valuable player in the NHL All-Star game?

15 How many times did the Winnipeg Jets win the Avco Cup as Champions of the World Hockey Association?

16 Name the four rearguards who have won the Norris Trophy as the NHL's best defenseman at least three consecutive times.

QUIZ 50

1 When asked who he thought was the dirtiest player in the National Hockey League he responded "Can I vote for myself?". Name him.

2 Awarded a National Hockey League franchise to begin the 1992-93 season, who did the Ottawa Senators select with their first choice (2nd overall) in the 1992 NHL Entry Draft?

3 Who holds the single season record for points by a defensman for both the Edmonton Oilers and the Pittsburgh Penguins?

4 Who has participated in the most NHL All-Star games as a defenseman?

5 Who was the first recipient of the Lester B. Pearson Award presented to the NHL's outstanding player as judged by the National Hockey League's Player Association?

6 Who was the last man to be both coach and general manager of the Stanley Cup Champions?

7 What nation won the World Junior Hockey Championships a record seven times in succession?

8 Name the only two players in NHL history to score at least 50 goals and record at least 100 points in their NHL rookie year.

9 Who is the only player to score over 500 NHL goals as a member of the St. Louis Blues?

10 In 1962, the first Bud Light NHL All-Star Game MVP Award was first presented. Who was the first player to win the Award?

11 The Florida Panthers have had the first selection in the NHL Entry Draft only once in the team's history. Who did the Panthers choose with their only number one selection in the Draft?

12 Name the Hall of fame netminder who was known as the "Chicoutimi Cucumber"?

13 Who holds the National Hockey League record for the most goals scored by a rookie defenseman in one season?

14 To whom was Prime Minister Pierre Trudeau referring when he said "Rarely has the career of an athlete been so exemplary"?

15 For which NHL team did the legendary Bobby Hull play the final game of his NHL career?

16 Name the only one of the Original Six NHL teams that has not had a player win the James Norris Trophy as the NHL's outstanding defenseman.

QUIZ 51

1 Who was the first player to play at least 20 seasons in the National Hockey League?

2 Gordie Howe of the Detroit Red Wings was the first player in NHL history to score 1500 points in his career. Who was next to reach the 1500 point plateau?

3 Name the first team in NHL history to win at least 50 regular season games, four years in succession.

4 Name the Sault Ste. Marie, Ontario native who was fittingly nicknamed "Sweet Lou from the Soo"?

5 Who is the only player in league history to win the Lady Byng Trophy as the NHL's most gentlemanly player with three different teams?

6 The Atlanta Flames began play in the National Hockey League in the 1972-73 season. Who coached the Flames in their inaugural season?

7 Who holds the NHL record for the most career power-play goals in the Stanley Cup Playoffs?

8 On February 10th, 1960, the Toronto Maple Leafs sent Marc Reaume to the Detroit Red Wings in a trade that shook the hockey world. Who did the Maple Leafs acquire in exchange for Reaume?

9 The Hartford Whalers of the 1980s featured a forward line known as the "FTD" line. Name the three members of this prolific scoring line.

10 Who was the last member of the Toronto Maple Leafs to win the Calder Memorial Trophy as the NHL's rookie of the year?

11 Who is the career leading playoff goal scorer among players who have not won a Stanley Cup Championship?

12 How many times have the Chicago Blackhawks won the Stanley Cup?

13 Name the only two defenseman in National Hockey League history to score 40 or more goals in a single regular season.

14 Name the Toronto Maple Leaf legend who is the only man to be inducted into three sports Hall of Fames.

15 Who is the only member of the Montreal Canadiens to lead the National Hockey League in goal scoring five times?

16 Who was the first rookie in NHL history to record at least 100 points in a single season?

QUIZ 52

1 Name the team that holds the record for the longest single season win streak in National Hockey League history.

2 Name the five National Hockey League goaltenders who have had their number 1 retired.

3 Who was the first goaltender to be selected the most valuable player in the NHL All-Star game?

4 Who is the only member of the Vancouver Canucks to win the Lester B. Pearson Award as the NHL's most valuable player as selected by the members of the National Hockey League Players Association?

5 Name the perennial NHL all-star who was once dubbed "Dawdling Doug"?

6 Game 6 of the 1964 Stanley Cup Fianl between the Detroit Red Wings and the Toronto Maple Leafs is considered to be one of the best playoff games in National Hockey League history. Name the Maple Leaf who scored the overtime marker in a 4-3 victory over the Red Wings thus forcing a seventh and deciding game.

7 Who were the first European-trained siblings to be chosen in the first round of the NHL Entry Draft in the same season?

8 Who holds the National Hockey League career record for the most games played in the Stanley Cup Playoffs?

9 With which Quebec Major Junior Hockey League team did Mike Bossy play his major junior hockey?

10 Who was the first referee to officiate in 1000 National Hockey League games?

11 Who was the first team to win the Stanley Cup despite the fact that they finished the regular season with a losing record?

12 With which team did Paul Coffey play the final game of his National Hockey League career?

13 Who is the only Edmonton Oiler goalkeeper to win the Vezina Trophy as the NHL's best netminder?

14 Name the only three players in NHL history to score at least 50 goals in a season, in 50 games or less, more than once during their careers.

15 Who is the only player in NHL history to score three overtime goals in a single game?

16 Name the Hockey Hall of Fame member who won the Lady Byng Memorial Trophy as the NHL's most gentlemanly player an astonishing seven times in an eight year period, prompting the National Hockey League to give him permanent possession of the award.

QUIZ 53

1 Name the diminutive NHL centerman who was nicknamed "Little Beaver"?

2 Who is the only member of the Detroit Red Wings to lead the National Hockey League in goal scoring at least five times?

3 Who was the first goaltender to win 400 games or more with one National Hockey League team?

4 Name the only two of the six Sutter brothers who were able to garner a Stanley Cup ring during their NHL playing days.

5 Name the only three members of the Edmonton Oilers to score five goals in a single NHL game.

6 The NHL record for the most career points by a goaltender stands at 48. Who holds this record?

7 Who is the only member of the Philadelphia Flyers to win the Hart Memorial Trophy as the NHL's most valuable player two consecutive times?

8 On March 13th, 1996, the Toronto Maple Leafs traded Kenny Jonsson, Darby Hendrickson, Sean Haggarty and their first choice in the 1997 NHL Entry Draft to the New York Islanders. Who did the Islanders send to the Maple Leafs to complete the trade?

9 Name the only rookie in NHL history to score at least 30 power-play goals in a single regular season.

10 Who is the only defenseman in National Hockey League history to record at least 100 points in a season for two different teams?

11 When asked what it was like to drink champagne from the Stanley Cup, who replied "Tastes like horse pee from a tin cup"?

12 On February 7th, 1976, Darryl Sittler of the Toronto Maple Leafs established an NHL record by recording ten points in a single game. Name the goaltender victimized by Sittler on his historic night.

13 Who are the only two members of the Detroit Red Wings to win the Frank J. Selke Trophy as the NHL's best defensive forward?

14 Who did Dale Hunter of the Washington Capitals slam into the boards in a Stanley Cup Playoff game on April 28th, 1993, thus earning a 21-game suspension by the National Hockey League?

15 Who has coached the most teams in National Hockey League history?

16 Who was the first player in NHL history to record at least 100 points in six consecutive seasons?

QUIZ 54

1 The Florida Panthers have had the first selection in the NHL Entry Draft just once in the franchise's history. Who did the Panthers select with their only number one pick?

2 Name the two members of the Toronto Maple Leafs to have their jerseys retired by the team.

3 On April 9th, 1987, Wayne Gretzky of the Edmonton Oilers recorded his 177th Stanley Cup playoff point to move into first place on the all-time playoff scoring list. Who held the record prior to "The Great One"?

4 Name the All-Star defenseman who was often referred to as "Big Bird"?

5 Who is the only Russian-born NHLer to be inducted into the Hockey Hall of Fame?

6 With which team did Pavel Bure play the final game of his National Hockey League career?

7 Name the only four players in National Hockey League history to win the Art Ross Memorial Trophy as the NHL's leading scorer at least four consecutive times.

8 Since 1967, how many times has the National Hockey League expanded its membership?

9 How many times has Sweden captured the Olympic Gold Medal in hockey?

10 Name the only two goaltenders in NHL history to be members of a record six Stanley Cup Championship teams.

11 To whom was Chicago Blackhawks general manager Tommy Ivan referring when he said, "Break another seat in practice and it's coming out of your paycheck"?

12 Name the Philadelphia Flyers star of the 1980s who was known as "The Sultan of Slot".

13 Who is the only forward to win the Conn Smythe Memorial Trophy as the most valuable player in the Stanley Cup Playoffs in consecutive seasons?

14 Name the team that holds the National Hockey League record for the most points in a single regular season.

15 Name the player that the Montreal Canadiens sought so frantically that they were prompted to purchase the entire Quebec Hockey League to obtain his services.

16 Name the three members of the Toronto Maple Leafs "Hound Line" who briefly skated together during the 1980s.

1 Who did the Buffalo Sabres name as their first coach in their history?

2 How many times have the Ottawa Senators won the Stanley Cup since the formation of the National Hockey League in 1917?

3 Who was the first goaltender in NHL history to actually shoot and score a goal in a regular season game?

4 Who was the first player to appear in 200 Stanley Cup Playoff games in his career?

5 With what nickname was much-traveled goaltender Gary Smith saddled?

6 Who was the coach of the Quebec Nordiques when they began NHL play in the 1979-80 season?

7 Gordie Howe was the first player in NHL history to score 600 goals in his career. Who was the next player to attain this lofty total?

8 On November 7th, 1975, the Boston Bruins traded Phil Esposito and Carol Vadnais to the New York Rangers. Who did the Bruins receive in exchange from the Rangers?

9 Only one rookie in National Hockey League history recorded 100 points in his first NHL season and failed to win the Calder Memorial Trophy as the league's rookie of the year. Name him?

10 Name the two Chicago Blackhawk goaltenders who have their sweaters retired by the team.

11 Name the only two members of the Washington Capitals to win the Vezina Trophy as the outstanding goaltender in the National Hockey League.

12 Name the Detroit Red Wing "tough guys" of the late 1980s and early 1990s who were known as "The Bruise Brothers".

13 In 1979-80, Wayne Gretzky tied for the NHL lead in scoring with 137 points. Who was awarded the Art Ross Trophy over Gretzky, on the basis of scoring more goals in the season?

14 Who received the most career penalty minutes in the short history of the World Hockey Association?

15 Name the three members of the Boston Bruins to be named the most valuable player in the NHL All-Star game.

16 Name the diminutive NHL left winger who was dubbed "The Little Giant" and "The Mighty Atom".

1 Who was the first player in NHL history to score at least 50 goals in a season six consecutive times?

2 Who is the youngest man to coach a National Hockey League team?

3 In game 6 of the 1972 Canada/Russia Summit Series, which Team Canada member broke the ankle of Russian star Valery Kharlamov?

4 The Minnesota Wild were awarded an NHL franchise to begin the 2000-01 season. Who did the Wild choose with their first selection in the 2000 NHL Entry Draft?

5 Who is the only member of the Los Angeles Kings to win the Calder Memorial Trophy as the National Hockey League's rookie of the year?

6 Who was the last goaltender to be selected to the NHL's First All-Star Team in his rookie season?

7 In 1994, an NHL lockout of players caused the cancellation of 468 regular season games. How many games did each team play in this lockout shortened season?

8 Who holds the Calgary Flames franchise record for the most points in a single regular season?

9 Who is the only defenseman to win the Lester B. Pearson Award as the NHL's outstanding player as selected by the National Hockey League Players Association?

10 By what two nicknames was Detroit Red Wing legend Ted Lindsay known?

11 Name the only two members of the Quebec Nordiques to score five goals in a single NHL game.

12 Who was the last member of the Detroit Red Wings to win the Vezina Trophy?

13 What was the name of the short-lived San Diego franchise in the World Hockey Association?

14 Who is the only goaltender in NHL history to win over 200 NHL regular season games with two different teams?

15 When Wayne Gretzky scored his 802nd goal of his NHL career he broke Gordie Howe's record of 801. Howe had broken Maurice Richard's record of 544, decades earlier. Whose record did Richard eclipse when he scored his 325th NHL goal on November 8th, 1952?

16 On March 7th, 1988, the St. Louis Blues traded Rob Ramage and Rick Walmsley to the Calgary Flames. Who did the Flames send to the Blues to complete the trade?

1 Who is the only member of the Pittsburgh Penguins to win the Calder Memorial Trophy as the NHL's rookie of the year?

2 With which team did Wendel Clark play the final game of his National Hockey League career?

3 Name the last NHL team to win at least 50 games in a regular season four consecutive times.

4 Who was known as "The Golden Jet"?

5 Name the only player in NHL history to win the Stanley Cup four times with two different teams.

6 Name the only two goaltenders in NHL history to capture the Hart Memorial Trophy as the NHL's most valuable player and the Vezina Trophy as the league's best goalkeeper in the same season.

7 Who is the oldest player in National Hockey League history to score 50 goals in a single regular season?

8 Who was the first coach in NHL history to win 500 regular season games with one team?

9 Name the member of the Hockey Hall of Fame whose aggressive style and scoring prowess earned him the nickname "Digging Dicker"?

10 What was the name of the Vancouver franchise in the World Hockey Association?

11 Who was the first member of the New York Rangers to record at least 100 points in a single NHL season?

12 The New York Islanders joined the NHL in 1972. Who did the Islanders select with their first choice of the 1972 NHL Entry Draft?

13 Who is the only player in NHL history to finish in the top 5 in National Hockey League scoring an incredible 20 seasons in succession?

14 Name the netminder who lost an NHL record 352 games during his Hall of Fame career.

15 In 1992, for the first time in NHL history Europeans were selected first and second overall in the National Hockey League Entry Draft. Name the first two players taken in the 1992 Draft.

16 Who is the only member of the Chicago Blackhawks to win the Art Ross Memorial Trophy as the NHL's leading scorer in back to back seasons?

QUIZ 58

1 Name the only two NHL goaltenders to record over 20 career shutouts in the Stanley Cup Playoffs.

2 Who is the only player in National Hockey League history to win the Conn Smythe Memorial Trophy as the Stanley Cup Playoffs' most valuable player and the following season capture the Calder Memorial Trophy as the NHL's rookie of the year?

3 Name the only three players in NHL history to record over 500 career points with two different teams.

4 Who was the last member of the Detroit Red Wings to record at least 100 points in a single NHL regular season?

5 Name the only defenseman to play 24 seasons in the National Hockey League.

6 The Toronto Maple Leafs began playing their home games at Maple Leaf Gardens in 1931. Where did the Maple Leafs call home prior to moving into the Gardens?

7 Who was the first goaltender to win the Lester B. Pearson Award as the NHL's outstanding player as voted by the National Hockey League Players Association?

8 Name the NHL superstar who once noted "All professional athletes are bilingual. They speak English and profanity".

9 Who is the highest scoring European-trained player in National Hockey League history?

10 By what nickname was stellar goaltender Terry Sawchuk known?

11 Name the four players who scored the 500th goal of their NHL careers while members of the Montreal Canadiens?

12 Who holds the record for the most points in a single NHL All-Star game?

13 Raymond Bourque was the sole captain of the Boston Bruins from 1988-89 until 1999-2000. Who succeeded Bourque as Boston's captain?

14 On August 9th, 1988, the Edmonton Oilers and the Los Angeles Kings were involved in what many consider to be the biggest trade in NHL history. The Oilers sent the Kings, Wayne Gretzky, Marty McSorley and Mike Krushelnyski. Whom did the Oilers receive in return?

15 Who is the only European-trained player to win the Calder Memorial Trophy as the NHL's rookie of the year to also capture the Hart Memorial Trophy as the NHL's most valuable player later in his career?

16 Who was the first player in NHL history to score at least 20 goals for five different teams?

1 Name the only player in NHL history to lead the league in goals, assists, points and penalty minutes in a season at least once?

2 Who was the first player in NHL history to record at least 60 assists in a single regular season?

3 Who was voted the most valuable player of the 1984 Canada Cup?

4 Who holds the single season record for points by a defenseman for both the Buffalo Sabres and the WInnipeg Jets/Phoenix Coyotes franchises?

5 Since 1962, only one player has been selected the most valuable player in the NHL All-Star Game in back to back seasons. Name him.

6 Who did Philadelphia Flyer head coach Fred Shero call "The Perfect Captain"?

7 Name the father and son duo who were members of a combined nine Stanley Cup Championship teams.

8 From 1981 until 2001, only three players had their name inscribed on the Art Ross Trophy as the NHL's leading scorer. Name them.

9 Name the only two players who have scored their 500th NHL career goal while members of the New York Rangers.

10 Who was the last player to record at least one point in 30 consecutive NHL games?

11 How many times did the Montreal Maroons capture the Stanley Cup since the formation of the National Hockey League in 1917?

12 Who was the first member of the St. Louis Blues to score 50 goals in a single NHL season?

13 Wayne Gretzky holds the NHL record for the most career goals in the Stanley Cup Playoffs with 122. Who has scored the most playoff goals with one team?

14 With which Quebec Major Junior Hockey League team did Sidney Crosby play his major junior hockey?

15 The World Hockey Association commenced play in 1972. Name the team that captured the Avco Cup as WHA Champion, in the league's first year of operation.

16 Name the three players who made up the Pittsburgh Penguins "Option Line".

1 Who holds the National Hockey League rookie goaltending record for the longest undefeated streak from the beginning of a career?

2 What was the nickname given to the Boston Bruins for the better part of the 1970s?

3 Who was the first rookie to lead the National Hockey League in goal scoring?

4 Wayne Gretzky won the Lester B. Pearson Award as the outstanding player in the NHL as voted by the National Hockey League Players Association, four consecutive times, from 1982 until 1985. Name the only other player to win the Award as many as three times in succession?

5 Who was the first player to win the Hart Memorial Trophy as the NHL's most valuable player in back to back seasons?

6 Who holds the Toronto Maple Leafs record for the most points by a defenseman in a single NHL season?

7 Name the only European-trained player to reach the 1000 point mark in his NHL career in under 700 games.

8 Who was the coach of the Chicago Blackhawks the last time they won the Stanley Cup?

9 Who is the only goaltender to be named to the NHL's First All-Star Team with three different teams?

10 Who was the last member of the Detroit Red Wings to lead the National Hockey League in goal scoring?

11 Name the three members of the Edmonton Oilers to have won the Conn Smythe Memorial Trophy as the NHL's most valuable player in the Stanley Cup Playoffs.

12 Who is the only member of the Washington Capitals to win the Frank J. Selke Trophy as the NHL's best defensive forward?

13 Name the goaltending great who was given the nickname "Cheesie".

14 Name the only player in NHL history to score four or more goals in a single playoff game, three times in his career.

15 Who is the only member of the San Jose Sharks to win the Calder Memorial Trophy as the NHL's rookie of the year?

16 Name the player who appeared in all of his team's games for nine straight season, establishing a then NHL record of 630 consecutive games played.

1 With which franchise did Doug Gilmour play the final game of his National Hockey League career?

2 Who was the first European-trained player to play on a Stanley Cup Championship team?

3 Name the classy centerman who was known as "Le Gros Bill".

4 Name the only three players in NHL history to win the Calder Trophy, Hart Trophy, Art Ross Trophy and Conn Smythe Trophy at least once during their careers.

5 Who is the only player in NHL history to average over two goals a game in a single season?

6 Who won the inaugural World Cup of Hockey in 1996?

7 Name the only two goaltenders in history to be named to the NHL's First All-Star Team four years in succession.

8 Name the only two players in NHL history to record at least eight points in a single game, twice in the same season.

9 To whom was Montreal Canadiens coach Dick Irvin referring, when he said "When 'Rocket' Richard hangs up his skates, that youngster will take over as the greatest player in the NHL"?

10 Name the only player in NHL history to win the Lester B. Pearson Award as the league's outstanding player, as voted by the National Hockey League Players Association, with two different teams.

11 Name the last team to win the Stanley Cup despite the fact that they finished the NHL regular season sub .500.

12 The Vancouver Canucks began NHL play in the 1970-71 season. Who was the first coach of the Canucks?

13 Who is known as "Alexander the Gr8"?

14 Who is the only member of the Colorado Avalanche to win the Maurice "Rocket" Richard Trophy as the NHL's leading goal scorer?

15 Who was voted the most valuable player of the 1996 World Cup of Hockey?

16 Name the three major junior hockey leagues that make up the Canadian Hockey League.

QUIZ 62

1 Name the United States-born player who has recorded the most career NHL points among Americans.

2 Name the only three players in history to be active players in the National Hockey League and honored members of the Hockey Hall of Fame.

3 Name the only member of the Dallas Stars to win the Frank J. Selke Trophy as the NHL's outstanding defensive forward.

4 Who is the all-time leading point producer among NHL players who has never had his name inscribed on the Stanley Cup?

5 Name the only two forwards to be selected to the NHL's First All-Star Team seven seasons in succession.

6 Who has won the most Stanley Cup rings as a player in National Hockey League history.

7 Name the only two sets of brothers to win the National Hockey League scoring title.

8 Who was the last player to lead the National Hockey League in goal scoring with two different teams?

9 Name the NHL enforcer who was often referred to as "Knuckles".

10 Who holds the NHL record for the longest consecutive game point scoring streak in a single Stanley Cup Playoff year?

11 How many times have the Montreal Canadiens won the Stanley Cup since the formation of the National Hockey League in 1917?

12 Who played in the most regular season games in the history of the World Hockey Association?

13 Bobby Orr of the Boston Bruins won the James Norris Trophy as the NHL's best defenseman eight consecutive times from 1968 until 1975. Name the player who won the 1967 Norris Trophy, Orr's rookie season in the NHL.

14 Name the Montreal Canadiens general manager who orchestrated the trade that led to the Habitants selecting Guy Lafleur with the first choice of the 1971 NHL Entry Draft.

15 Name the only two players in NHL history to score three overtime goals in a single Stanley Cup Playoff campaign.

16 Who was the first European-trained player to be named to the National Hockey League's First All-Star Team?

1 Name the goaltender who holds the modern NHL record for the longest shutout streak during the regular season.

2 In 1970-71, the Boston Bruins became the first team in NHL history to boast the top four point producers in the league. Name the Bruins who finished 1,2,3,4 in scoring that season.

3 Who was named the most valuable player of the 2004 World Cup of Hockey?

4 Name the NHL head coach who invoked "Pyramid Power" in an effort to help his team.

5 Who was the first rookie in NHL history to record at least 70 points in a single season?

6 Name the veteran of twenty NHL seasons known as "Stumpy".

7 Who did *Hockey News* name as the greatest hockey player of the 20th century?

8 Name the NHL team that posted "to you from failing hands we throw the torch; be yours to hold it high" in their dressing room?

ANSWERS

QUIZ 1 ANSWERS

1 Jean Beliveau was the first recipient of the Conn Smythe Memorial Trophy in 1965.

2 Phil and Tony Esposito were named to the NHL All-Star Team in 1970 and again in 1972.

3 Bobby Hull of the Chicago Blackhawks led the NHL in goal scoring in 1959-60, 1961-62, 1963-64, 1965-66, 1966-67, 1967-68 and 1968-69.

4 Raymond Bourque scored 410 times during his NHL career with the Boston Bruins and the Colorado Avalanche.

5 The Montreal Canadiens appeared in the Stanley Cup Finals an incredible 10 years in succession, from 1951 until 1960.

6 Eric Lindros, John LeClair and Mikael Renberg formed the Flyers "Legion of Doom" line.

7 George "Punch" Imlach was behind the bench for the Leafs for their Stanley Cup victories in 1962, 1963, 1964 and 1967.

8 Lecavalier played for Rimouski Oceanic from 1996 until 1998 while Richards played for the Oceanic from 1997 until 2000.

9 The Leafs selected Wendel Clark with the first overall pick of the 1985 NHL Entry Draft.

10 Andrew Raycroft of the Boston Bruins captured the Calder Memorial Trophy in 2004.

11 The Vancouver Canucks and the Buffalo Sabres joined the National Hockey League at the beginning of the 1970-71 season.

12 Gordie Howe earned the moniker "Mr. Hockey" for his dominance of all phases of the game during his illustrious career.

13 Wayne Gretzky scored 92 times during the 1981-82 season and 87 times in the 1983-84 campaign. Mario Lemieux tallied 85 goals in the 1988-89 season while Brett Hull scored 86 times during the 1990-91 schedule.

14 Scott Niedermayer became the only Devil to win the James Norris Trophy when he won the award in 2004.

15 Sergei Fedorov of the Detroit Red Wings was the first European-trained player to be voted the winner of the Hart Memorial Trophy when he was named the League's MVP in the strike shortened 1993-94 season.

16 Bernie Parent of the Philadelphia Flyers was named the Stanley Cup Playoffs' MVP in both 1974 and 1975.

QUIZ 2 ANSWERS

1 Raymond Bourque and Denis Potvin each had nine 20 goal seasons during their Hall of Fame careers.

2 Guy Lafleur led the NHL in scoring in the 1977-78 season with 132 points on 60 goals and 72 assists.

3 The Bruins acquired Phil Esposito, Ken Hodge and Fred Stanfield from the Hawks. The trio would help turn the Bruins into Stanley Cup contenders.

4 Glenn Hall was selected to the NHL's First All-Star Team 7 times and on 4 other occasions was selected to NHL's Second All-Star Team.

5 Messier played 5 games with the Indianapolis Racers of the WHA during the 1978-79 season. He also played 47 games for the Cincinnati Stingers that same year.

6 Mike Bossy of the New York Islanders scored at least 50 goals in a season from 1977 until 1986.

7 The Detroit Red Wings have captured a total of 10 Stanley Cup titles in the franchise's history. The Wings won their first Cup in 1936 and last took home hockey's top prize in 2002.

8 George Armstrong was the captain of the Toronto Maple Leafs for a record 11 seasons. He earned the nickname due to his native descent.

9 Bobby Hull scored at least 50 goals five times in in his NHL career and four times notched 50 or more during his time in the World Hockey Association. Blaine Stoughton scored 52 times for the 1976-77 Cincinnati Stingers of the WHA and scored at least 50 twice as a member of the NHL's Hartford Whalers.

10 The Penguins selected Mario Lemieux first overall in 1984, Marc-Andre Fleury first in 2003 and Sidney Crosby number one in 2005.

11 Canada's Phil Esposito scored 7 goals and added 6 assists for 13 points to lead all scorers in the 1972 Summit Series.

12 Gretzky played for the Edmonton Oilers from 1979 until 1988, the Los Angeles Kings from 1988 until 1996, the St. Louis Blues in 1996 and the New York Rangers from 1996 until 1999.

13 Bobby Orr was just 30 years of age when he was inducted into the Hockey Hall of Fame in 1979.

14 Ken Morrow was a member of the United States Olympic team that captured gold at the 1980 Olympic Games in Lake Placid, New York. He would then join the New York Islanders and help them to the 1980 Stanley Cup title.

15 On June 17th, 1989, the Quebec Nordiques chose Swedish born Mats Sundin with the first pick of the 1989 NHL Entry Draft.

16 Terry Sawchuk was the first NHL netminder to record 400 wins in the regular season. Sawchuk would go on to win 447 games during his 21 seasons in the league.

QUIZ 3 ANSWERS

1 Goaltender Roger Crozier was the last Red Wing to win the Calder Trophy when he captured the Award in 1965.

2 Mario Lemieux of the Pittsburgh Penguins scored 13 shorthanded goals during the 1988-89 season, to establish the record.

3 Jean Ratelle, Rod Gilbert and Vic Hadfield formed the Rangers GAG Line (Goal a Game).

4 Brad Richards won the Conn Smythe Trophy in 2004, leading the Lightning to their first Stanley Cup title.

5 The Minnesota North Stars, St. Louis Blues, Philadelphia Flyers, Oakland Seals, Los Angeles Kings and the Pittsburgh Penguins joined the NHL in 1967.

6 Jacques Demers of the Detroit Red Wings won the Jack Adams Award in both 1987 and 1988.

7 Raymond Bourque totaled 1579 points in his 22 NHL seasons and Paul Coffey recorded 1531 points in his 21 years in the league.

8 Tony Esposito of the Chicago Blackhawks shut out the opposition 15 times in the 1969-70 season to establish the record.

9 Teemu Selanne of the Anaheim Mighty Ducks scored 47 goals to capture the inaugural Richard Trophy in 1999.

10 In 1995, Eric Lindros became the last Flyer to win the Hart Memorial Trophy.

11 Red Horner of the Toronto Maple Leafs led the NHL in penalty minutes from the 1932-33 season until his retirement after the 1939-40 season.

12 Gilmour played for the Cornwall Royals of the OHL from 1980 until 1983.

13 Stan Mikita of the Chicago Blackhawks captured all three Trophies in 1967 and again in 1968.

14 Best known as a Toronto Maple Leaf, Salming played the final 49 games of his NHL career with the Detroit Red Wings during the 1989-90 season.

15 The Atlanta Thrashers chose Ilya Kovalchuk with the first pick of the 2001 NHL Entry Draft.

16 Toronto Maple Leaf defenceman Tim Horton was the only player to be named to the 1963-64 NHL First All-Star Team who was not a member of the Blackhawks.

QUIZ 4 ANSWERS

1 Patrick Roy was 20 years of age when he won the 1986 Conn Smythe Trophy as a member of the Stanley Cup Champion, Montreal Canadiens.

2 Cherry coached the Boston Bruins from 1974 until he was fired in 1979 and was behind the bench for the Colorado Rockies for the 1979-80 NHL campaign.

3 Harry Lumley was just 17 years of age when he made his NHL debut as a member of the Detroit Red Wings during the 1943-44 season.

4 Rick MacLeish became the first Flyer to score 50 goals when he achieved the feat during the 1972-73 season.

5 Mike Bossy of the New York Islanders tallied at least 60 goals during the 1978-79, 1980-81, 1981-82, 1982-83 and 1985-86 regular seasons.

6 Bobby Orr scored 46 goals and added 89 assists for 135 points to lead all scorers during the 1974-75 season.

7 The Detroit Red Wings won a record setting 62 games in the 1995-96 NHL regular season.

8 Theo Fleury of the Calgary Flames scored 3 shorthanded goals in a 8-4 victory over the St. Louis Blues on March 9th, 1991.

9 Best known as a member of the Toronto Maple Leafs, Dave Keon appeared to play the game in constant motion.

10 Wayne Gretzky of the Edmonton Oilers had at least one point in 51 consecutive games in the 1983-84 season while Mario Lemieux went 46 games with at least a point for the 1989-90 Pittsburgh Penguins.

11 Defenseman Brian Leetch won the Conn Smythe Trophy in 1994 leading the Rangers to their first Stanley Cup title in fifty years.

12 Jari Kurri was inducted into the Hockey Hall of Fame in 2001, becoming the first Finland born member of the Hall.

13 Imlach was speaking of Rogatien Vachon of the Montreal Canadiens. Vachon would go on to have a stellar NHL career.

14 Gilbert Perreault was taken first overall by the Sabres in the 1970 NHL Entry Draft.

15 Alexander Mogilny won the Lady Byng Trophy in 2003.

16 Gordie Howe, Ted Lindsay and Sid Abel led the Red Wings to four Stanley Cup Championships in the 1950s.

QUIZ 5 ANSWERS

1 Sidney Crosby of the Pittsburgh Penguins was 4 months short of his nineteenth birthday when he concluded the 2005-06 NHL season with 39 goals and 63 assists for 102 points.

2 Dave Schultz of the Philadelphia Flyers spent a record 472 minutes in the penalty box during the 1974-75 season.

3 Andy Brown of the Pittsburgh Penguins during the 1973-74 season, was the last goaltender to play an NHL game without a facemask.

4 Bobby Orr of the Boston Bruins had 102 assists in the 1970-71 season and had 90 helpers during the 1973-74 campaign. Paul Coffey of the Edmonton Oilers registered 90 assists in the 1985-86 season.

5 Brett Hull of the St. Louis Blues led the NHL in goals scored from the 1989-90 season until the 1991-92 season.

6 Mats Naslund of the Montreal Canadiens set the All-Star Game record of 5 assists in the 1988 contest.

7 Danny Gallivan began announcing Montreal Canadiens games on radio in 1952. He would be associated with the Canadiens for over 30 years and cover over 1800 Habs games.

8 The Edmonton Oilers, Hartford Whalers, Quebec Nordiques and Winnipeg Jets joined the NHL from the WHA for the 1979-80 season.

9 Randy Carlyle of the Penguins, won the Norris Trophy in 1981, out-polling the New York Islanders' Denis Potvin.

10 Yzerman was a member of the OHL's Peterborough Petes from 1981 until 1983.

11 The Bruins acquired Johnny Bucyk and cash from the Red Wings for goaltender Terry Sawchuk.

12 Bobby Carpenter of the Washington Capitals scored 53 times during the 1984-85 season, to become the first American to score at least 50 goals in an NHL season.

13 Lou Fontinato, who played for the New York Rangers and Montreal Canadiens during his nine-year NHL career.

14 Bobby Orr of the Boston Bruins won the Hart Memorial Trophy from 1970 until 1972 while Wayne Gretzky of the Edmonton Oilers took home the Trophy an incredible eight years in succession from 1980 until 1987.

15 Forwards Gary Roberts and Joe Nieuwendyk signed two year deals with the Panthers on August 1st, 2005.

16 Mike Gartner scored 30 or more goals in a season from 1979-80 until 1993-94.

QUIZ 6 ANSWERS

1 On October 16th, 1946, Howe appeared in his first NHL game as a member of the Detroit Red Wings wearing sweater number 17.

2 Neely played three uneventful seasons with the Vancouver Canucks from 1983 until 1986. He was traded to the Bruins for Barry Pederson on June 6th, 1986.

3 Steve Larmer, whose consecutive game streak spanned 11 NHL seasons, from 1982 until 1993.

4 Bill Durnan of the Montreal Canadiens had the best goals against average in the NHL from 1943-44 until 1946-47.

5 Rookie Mike Bossy of the New York Islanders scored 53 times during the 1977-78 regular season.

6 Bryan Trottier scored five times in a game on December 23rd, 1978, and duplicated the feat on February 13th, 1982. John Tonelli scored five times in a game on January 6th, 1981.

7 With the first picks the Nordiques chose Mats Sundin in 1989, Owen Nolan in 1990 and Eric Lindros in 1991.

8 In 1954, Red Kelly of the Detroit Red Wings became the first recipient of the James Norris Trophy.

9 Glenn Hall, arguably the greatest netminder in NHL history. He played 906 NHL games during his fantastic career.

10 Joe Thornton scored 36 goals and added 65 assists for 101 points during the 2002-03 season.

11 On December 11th, 1992, Gary Bettman became the NHL's first Commissioner. Prior to Bettman, the head of the NHL was known as President.

12 On April 4th, 1987, Denis Potvin of the New York Islanders became the first NHL rearguard to record 1000 points in his career. Potvin would go on to total 1052 points in his 1060 NHL games.

13 Reggie Leach of the Philadelphia Flyers won the Smythe Trophy in 1976. His Flyers were defeated by the Montreal Canadiens in the Cup Final in four straight games.

14 Al Arbour coached the New York Islanders to 739 victories in his 19 seasons with the club.

15 Guy Lapointe, Larry Robinson and Serge Savard were regarded as the best threesome of rearguards in the NHL in the 1970s.

16 Peter Stastny of the Quebec Nordiques in 1980-81 and Joe Juneau of the Boston Bruins in 1993-94 both recorded a rookie record 70 assists.

QUIZ 7 ANSWERS

1 Pat Burns won coach of the year honors in 1989 with the Montreal Canadiens, in 1993 with the Toronto Maple Leafs and in 1998 with the Boston Bruins.

2 Peter Forsberg led the NHL in scoring in 2002-03 with 29 goals and 77 assists for 106 points.

3 Marcel Dionne was voted the NHL's best player by the NHLPA in both 1979 and 1980.

4 Best known as the "Stratford Streak", Morenz was also known as the "Mitchell Meteor", the "Hurtling Hab" and the "Canadien Comet".

5 Jarome Iginla of the Calgary Flames won both the Art Ross Trophy and the Rocket Richard Trophy in the 2001-02 season.

6 Darryl Sittler scored 389 goals and added 527 assists for 916 points as a member of the Leafs from 1970 until 1982.

7 Raymond Bourque was selected to the NHL's First All-Star Team 13 times in his career while Doug Harvey was chosen 10 times to the league's first team.

8 Esposito played 13 games for the Montreal Canadiens during the 1968-69 season.

9 Chris Chelios was the first American to claim the Norris Trophy when he won the award in 1989 as a member of the Montreal Canadiens.

10 On March 23rd, 1952, Bill Mosienko of the Chicago Blackhawks scored 3 times in just 21 seconds in a 7-6 Hawks victory over the New York Rangers.

11 The Toronto Maple Leafs reeled off ten consecutive victories to begin the 1993-94 season.

12 Gretzky's teammate Esa Tikkanen got under the skin of opponents with his relentless checking and trash talking.

13 On March 2nd, 1969, Phil Esposito of the Boston Bruins became the first member of the NHL to reach 100 points in a season. Esposito would finish the year with a record 126 points.

14 Stan Mikita played his entire NHL career with the Blackhawks, a total of 1394 games in 22 seasons.

15 Mel Hill of the Boston Bruins scored three overtime goals in the 1939 Stanley Cup Semi-Finals against the New York Rangers thus earning the nickname "Sudden Death".

16 Brad Richards of the Tampa Bay Lightning scored seven game winning goals during the club's run to the Stanley Cup Championship in 2004.

QUIZ 8 ANSWERS

1 The Pittsburgh franchise was known as the Pirates. They finished out of the Playoffs in three of the five seasons that they were members of the NHL.

2 Famous for scoring the Series winning goal in the eighth game of the "Summit Series", Paul Henderson also scored the game winner in the sixth and seventh contests.

3 Dick Irvin lost in the Stanley Cup Final once with the Chicago Blackhawks, six times as coach of the Toronto Maple Leafs and on five occasions with the Montreal Canadiens.

4 Maurice "Rocket" Richard was runner-up for the Art Ross Trophy in 1945, 1947, 1951, 1954 and 1955.

5 Bobby Orr won the Conn Smythe Trophy in both 1970 and 1972 leading the Bruins to the Stanley Cup on both occasions.

6 The 1987-88 Calgary Flames saw Joe Nieuwendyk score 51 goals, Hakan Loob 50, Mike Bullard 48 and Joe Mullen 40.

7 The Penquins retired Michel Briere's sweater number 21. Briere died on April 13th, 1971, as a result of injuries he suffered in an automobile accident.

8 Jaromir Jagr of the Pittsburgh Penguins led the NHL in scoring in the strike shortened 1994-95 season with 32 goals and 38 assists for 70 points.

9 Eddie Johnston of the Boston Bruins played every minute of the 70-game schedule during the 1963-64 season.

10 Pronger played his junior hockey with the Peterborough Petes of the OHL from 1991 until 1993.

11 The Blackhawks sent Denis Savard to the Canadiens in the Chelios trade. Savard would win his only Stanley Cup ring with the Canadiens in 1993.

12 In 1969, Serge Savard of the Montreal Canadiens became the first defenseman to capture the Conn Smythe Trophy, helping the Habs to the Stanley Cup Championship.

13 Herb Brooks coached the Americans to the Olympic Gold Medal in the 1980 Games at Lake Placid, New York. The U.S. triumph became known as "The Miracle on Ice".

14 Johnny Bower and Terry Sawchuk were both outstanding in goal, leading the Leafs to their last Stanley Cup title.

15 Barrett Jackman won the Calder Trophy in 2003, the first Blue to win the Award.

16 Charlie Conacher, Joe Primeau and Harvey "Busher" Jackson formed perhaps the most dominant forward line in the NHL during the 1930s.

QUIZ 9 ANSWERS

1 Stephane Richer scored 51 times for the Canadiens during the 1989-90 season.

2 Bobby Orr of the Boston Bruins led the NHL in assists in 1969-70, 1970-71, 1971-72, 1973-74 and 1974-75.

3 Bernie Nicholls of the Kings scored to 2 goals and added 6 assists in a 9-3 victory over the Toronto Maple Leafs on December 1st, 1988.

4 Grant Fuhr of the St. Louis Blues set the record when he appeared in 79 of the team's 82 games during the 1995-96 regular season.

5 The Canucks acquired Markus Naslund from the Penguins, in what now must be considered an extremely one-sided deal.

6 Bobby Clarke of the Philadelphia Flyers won the Hart Trophy in 1973 becoming the first member of an expansion team to do so.

7 Bobby Hull scored 610 goals in his NHL career and added 303 more while a member of the Winnipeg Jets of the WHA.

8 Cherry played one game for the Boston Bruins during the 1955 Stanley Cup Playoffs.

9 George Hainsworth of the Montreal Canadiens recorded 22 shutouts in just 44 games during the 1928-29 regular season.

10 Harvey played 70 games for the expansion St. Louis Blues during the 1968-69 season.

11 On December 11th, 1977, Tom Bladon of the Philadelphia Flyers scored 4 goals and added 4 assists for 8 points to establish the record. Paul Coffey of the Edmonton Oilers equaled the mark on March 14th, 1986, when he recorded 8 points on 2 goals and 6 assists.

12 In 1974, Fred Shero of the Philadelphia Flyers became the first recipient of the Jack Adams Award.

13 Neal Broten of the Minnesota North Stars was the first U.S. born player to record 100 points in an NHL season. In the 1985-86 season, Broten scored 29 goals and assisted on 76 others for 105 points.

14 Jacques Plante, perhaps the most innovative and influential goalkeeper in NHL history.

15 The Sabres selected Gilbert Perreault with the first pick of the 1970 Entry Draft and chose Pierre Turgeon as number one in the 1987 Entry Draft.

16 Bob Probert of the Chicago Blackhawks scored the final goal at Maple Leaf Gardens when he beat Leaf netminder Curtis Joseph at 11:05 of the third period.

QUIZ 10 ANSWERS

1 Vic Hadfield was the first Ranger to score 50 times in a season when he notched exactly 50 during the 1971-72 campaign.

2 Alexander Mogilny of the Buffalo Sabres scored 76 times during the 1992-93 regular season.

3 Brian Bellows of the Minnesota North Stars was just 19 years of age when he was named the club's captain for the 1983-84 NHL season.

4 The Howes joined the WHA's Houston Aeros for the 1973-74 season and would continue to play together until Gordie's retirement at the conclusion of the 1979-80 NHL season.

5 Lindros played for the Oshawa Generals of the OHL from 1989-90 until 1991-92.

6 The Senators' Daniel Alfredsson won the Calder Memorial Trophy in 1996.

7 Hector "Toe" Blake won the Lady Byng in 1946 and Mats Naslund captured the Award in 1988.

8 The AHL championship trophy is the Calder Cup first awarded in 1936 -37 to the Syracuse Stars.

9 Wayne Gretzky won the Hart Trophy in 1989 out-polling Mario Lemieux of the Pittsburgh Penguins.

10 Dale Hunter recorded 1020 points and totaled 3565 penalty minutes in his 1407 games in the National Hockey League.

11 Pavel Bure of the Florida Panthers led the NHL in goal scoring in 1999-2000 with 58 goals and 2000-01 with 59.

12 Dave Andreychuk was the last Leaf to score at least 50 times in a season when he notched 53 during the 1993-94 schedule.

13 Patrick Roy of the Montreal Canadiens was in the net for all ten of the Habs overtime wins in the 1993 Stanley Cup playoffs.

14 Jim McKenny went on to have a lengthy career as a sports broadcaster on television in Toronto, after his retirement from hockey.

15 Ted Lindsay of the Detroit Red Wings scored three times for the Red Wings in a 7-1 victory over the NHL All-Stars during the 1950 All-Star Game.

16 The Philadelphia Flyers went undefeated from October 14th, 1979 until January 6th, 1980, a span of 35 games. The Flyers won 25 times and tied 10 others during their remarkable run.

QUIZ 11 ANSWERS

1 Al MacInnis won the Conn Smythe Trophy in 1989, leading the Flames to their only Stanley Cup Championship.

2 Ian Turnbull of the Toronto Maple Leafs scored five times, in a 9-1 victory over the Detroit Red Wings, on February 2nd, 1977.

3 Howie Morenz was selected as Canada's premier hockey player for the years 1901 to 1950.

4 The Leafs sent the extremely popular Lanny McDonald and Joel Quenneville to the Rockies for Hickey and Paiement.

5 Jose Theodore of the Montreal Canadiens won the Hart Trophy in 2002, the last goalie to win the Trophy.

6 Bob Gainey of the Montreal Canadiens was named the winner of the Selke Trophy from 1978 until 1981 inclusive.

7 Bryan Trottier, Mike Bossy and Clarke Gillies formed the Islanders "Trio Grande" line. All three would later be inducted into the Hockey Hall of Fame.

8 Mats Sundin recorded his 1000th point of his NHL career, when he scored a goal in a 3-2 Leaf victory over the Edmonton Oilers on March 10th, 2003.

9 The NHL took control of the Stanley Cup in 1926. In previous seasons, the winners of the now defunct Western or Pacific Coast Leagues would challenge the NHL champion in the Stanley Cup Final.

10 Goaltender Ed Belfour of the Blackhawks won the Calder Memorial Trophy in 1991.

11 Joe Nieuwendyk scored five times in a 8-3 Flames victory over the Winnipeg Jets, on January 11th, 1989.

12 On October 5th, 2005, the Ottawa Senators defeated the Toronto Maple Leafs 3-2, in the first NHL game to be decided via shootout.

13 Sakic played for the Swift Current Broncos of the WHL, scoring 148 goals in his two seasons there.

14 Dave Keon won the Conn Smythe Trophy in 1967, leading the Leafs to their fourth Stanley Cup of the decade.

15 In 1981, Czechoslovakia-born Peter Stastny of the Quebec Nordiques became the first European to win the Calder Memorial Trophy.

16 The Atlanta Thrashers joined the National Hockey League in 1999, making the NHL a 28 team league.

QUIZ 12 ANSWERS

1 On March 31st, 1991, Chris Nilan of the Boston Bruins received 6 minor penalties, 2 majors, one ten minute misconduct and one game misconduct in a game versus the Hartford Whalers.

2 Richard's, Montreal teammate Bernie Geoffrion recorded 75 points to win the 1954-55 scoring title. Richard would finish the season with 74 points.

3 Paul Coffey of the Oilers won the James Norris Trophy in both 1985 and 1986.

4 The pugnacious McKenzie was known simply as "Pie".

5 The Canucks acquired Todd Bertuzzi, Bryan McCabe and a 3rd round draft pick from the Islanders

6 Eddie Shore of the Boston Bruins won the Hart Trophy in 1933, 1935,1936 and 1938.

7 On January 2nd, 2000, Scotty Bowman became the first in the NHL to coach in five different decades. Bowman began as coach of the St. Louis Blues in 1967 and would end his coaching career with the Detroit Red Wings in 2002.

8 Howie Meeker of the Toronto Maple Leafs scored 5 times in a game on January 8th, 1947, and Don Murdoch of the New York Rangers duplicated the feat on October 12th, 1976.

9 Mike Bossy of the New York Islanders scored 17 goals and added 18 assists for 35 points in just 18 games in leading the Islanders to the 1981 Stanley Cup Championship.

10 Gilmour played for the St. Louis Blues from 1983 until 1988. He would makes stops in six other NHL cities during his career.

11 Rookie Terry Sawchuk of the Detroit Red Wings would set the record for wins in a season by an NHL goaltender, with 44 victories during the 1950-51 season.

12 Goaltender Ken Dryden was chosen the NHL's rookie of the year in 1972, the last Hab to be so honored.

13 The Rangers captured the Stanley Cup in 1928, 1933, 1940 and 1994 for a total of four Stanley Cup Championships.

14 Mark Recchi scored 53 goals and added 70 assists for 123 points during the 1992-93 season to establish the Flyer record.

15 Gordie Howe scored at least 20 goals in a season 22 times during his NHL career while Ron Francis tallied at least 20, 20 times.

16 Alexander Mogilny of the Buffalo Sabres scored 50 goals in his first 46 games of the 1992-93 season, while Cam Neely of the Boston Bruins recorded 50 goals in his first 44 games of the 1993-94 schedule.

QUIZ 13 ANSWERS

1 Ken Dryden's Montreal Canadiens defeated Dave Dryden's Buffalo Sabres 5-2 at the Montreal Forum. The goaltenders remain the only siblings to face each other in an NHL game.

2 Steve Yzerman of the Detroit Red Wings was just 22 years of age when he was named captain of the team in 1986. Yzerman was still the Red Wings captain at the close of the 2005-06 season, a span of 20 years.

3 Rick Vaive became the first Leaf to score 50 goals in a season when he scored 54 times during the 1981-82 season.

4 Scott Niedermayer played for the Kamloops Blazers of the WHL from 1989 until 1992.

5 On November 4th, 1962, Bill Gadsby of the Detroit Red Wings became the first NHL rearguard to reach 500 career points. Gadsby would finish his career with 568 points.

6 Dominik Hasek has been one of the most dominant goaltenders in the NHL for the better part of a decade.

7 The Detroit franchise was first known as the Cougars, from 1926 until 1930. The team then changed its name to the Falcons for the 1930-31 and 1931-32 NHL seasons.

8 Jacques Martin won the Jack Adams Award in 1999.

9 Dino Ciccarelli of the Minnesota North Stars scored 14 times during the 1981 Stanley Cup Playoffs, to establish the rookie record.

10 Jaromir Jagr is often compared to his former teammate Mario Lemieux. Jagr's first name can be rearranged to spell "Mario Jr.".

11 The 1988 Winter Olympic Games in Calgary, Alberta, were the first Games to feature professional players. The Soviet Union would capture the Gold Medal in these historic Games.

12 Gordie Howe won the Art Ross Trophy in 1962-63 accumulating a league leading 86 points on 38 goals and 48 assists.

13 Johnny Bower, who played on four Stanley Cup Champions as a member of the Toronto Maple Leafs.

14 In the 1969-70 NHL season, Bobby Orr of the Boston Bruins won the Hart, Art Ross, James Norris and Conn Smythe Trophies, becoming the first NHL player to win four individual awards in a single season.

15 The Canucks chose Dale Tallon from the Toronto Marlboroughs of the Ontario Hockey Association with the second overall selection of the 1970 NHL Entry Draft.

16 Richard Martin became the first Sabre to score 50 times in a season when he potted 52 during the 1973-74 schedule.

QUIZ 14 ANSWERS

1 Nicklas Lidstrom of the Detroit Red Wings became the first European to win the Conn Smythe Trophy, when he was the Playoff MVP in 2002.

2 The Detroit Red Wings selected Joe Murphy from Michigan State University with the first pick of the 1986 NHL Entry Draft.

3 The renowned Rene Lecavalier called the first televised game on the CBC, from the Montreal Forum, describing the action, in French.

4 Dave "Tiger" Williams was penalized a total of 3966 minutes in his 962 games in the NHL.

5 Eddie Shore of the Boston Bruins played one season (1926-27) with the Edmonton Eskimos of the Western Hockey League, thus earning his nickname.

6 On March 24th, 1936, Mud Bruneteau of the Detroit Red Wings scored after 116:30 minutes of overtime to give the Red Wings a 1-0 victory over the Montreal Maroons, in the longest game in NHL history.

7 In 1968, Claude Provost of the Montreal Canadiens was the first to win the Masterton Trophy.

8 Coffey's number 7 joined Wayne Gretzky's 99, Grant Fuhr's 31, Jari Kurri's 17, and Al Hamilton's number 3 in the rafters of the Rexall Place.

9 The Montreal Canadiens lost just 8 times in the 80 game schedule during the 1976-77 season.

10 Rick DiPietro became the first goaltender to taken first overall in the Entry Draft. DiPietro was chosen by the New York Islanders with the first pick of the 2000 Draft.

11 Camille "The Eel" Henry won the Calder Trophy in 1954 as a member of the New York Rangers.

12 Rookie Joe Nieuwendyk scored 51 goals in just 75 games during the 1987-88 NHL regular season.

13 Ted Kennedy was the last Leaf to capture the Hart Trophy when he won NHL MVP honors in 1955.

14 The Blackhawks called Chicago Stadium home for six and half decades.

15 Wayne Gretzky won the Ross Trophy seven years in succession from 1981 until 1987, while Gordie Howe from 1951 to 1954, Phil Esposito from 1971 to 1974 and Jaromir Jagr from 1998 to 2001, all won the Ross Trophy four times in a row.

16 Raymond Bourque totaled 17 points in his 19 All-Star appearances, to establish the record.

QUIZ 15 ANSWERS

1 Ted Lindsay was traded to the Blackhawks as punishment for his attempts to form an NHL's player union, while Glenn Hall would solve the Hawks goaltending woes for the next decade.

2 Steve Shutt scored 60 goals during the 1976-77 NHL regular season and Guy Lafleur duplicated the feat the following season.

3 Craig MacTavish was the last NHL'er to play without a helmet. MacTavish played over 1000 NHL games without a helmet.

4 Fred Shero coached the Flyers to their two consecutive Stanley Cup titles in 1975 and 1976.

5 Hector "Toe" Blake, Maurice "Rocket" Richard and Elmer Lach made up the Habs "Punch Line". All three would later become members of the Hockey Hall of Fame.

6 The Cleveland Barons and the Minnesota North Stars merged in 1978. The merged team played its home games in Minnesota as the North Stars.

7 Joe Sakic in 2001 and Peter Forsberg in 2003 are the only members of the Colorado Avalanche to win NHL MVP honors.

8 On March 3rd, 1968, Jean Beliveau of the Montreal Canadiens became the second NHLer to record 1000 points in his career.

9 Martin Brodeur of the New Jersey Devils captured the Vezina Trophy in both 2003 and 2004.

10 Modano played for the Prince Albert Raiders of the WHL from 1986 until 1989, scoring 118 goals as a member of the team.

11 Gilbert Perreault of the Buffalo Sabres was selected first overall in the 1970 Entry Draft and went on to win the Calder Trophy for the 1970-71 season.

12 Marc Tardif scored 316 goals during his WHA career, to establish the league record.

13 The Conn Smythe Trophy was captured by members of the New York Islanders from 1980 until 1983. Bryan Trottier in 1980, Butch Goring in1981, Mike Bossy in 1982 and Billy Smith in 1983 were all voted Playoff MVP.

14 Glenn Hall played every minute of 502 straight NHL games. Hall's streak began at the start of the 1955-56 season and continued through the first 12 games of the 1962-63 campaign. Most experts agree that this is the one NHL record that will never be broken.

15 Bernie Nicholls is the only King to score 70 times in a season. Nicholls potted 70 goals for the Kings in the 1988-89 season.

16 Swedish-born Ulf Sterner became the first European trained player to suit up for an NHL team when he appeared in four games during the 1964-65 season with the New York Rangers.

QUIZ 16 ANSWERS

1 On May 18th, 1986, Brian Skrudland of the Montreal Canadiens scored at the nine second mark of the first overtime period, in a 3-2 Hab victory over the Calgary Flames.

2 The Canucks' Pat Quinn captured the Jack Adams Award as NHL coach of the year, in 1992.

3 The first all-American Stanley Cup Final took place in 1929 as the Boston Bruins defeated the New York Rangers two games to none, to claim their first Stanley Cup Championship.

4 In 1970-71, Ed Giacomin became the last Rangers goalie to be named to the NHL's First All-Star Team.

5 Though possessing terrific defensive abilities, Allan Stanley was not noted for his skating prowess, hence the nickname "Snowshoes".

6 Guy Lafleur of the Montreal Canadiens held the record before Gretzky when he recorded at least one point in 28 straight games during the 1976-77 season.

7 Dale Hunter with 323 goals, Dave Hunter with 133 and Mark Hunter with 213, combined physical toughness with scoring ability during their NHL careers.

8 Cam Neely scored 50 times for the Bruins during the 1993-94 season.

9 Denis Potvin of the New York Islanders ended Orr's reign as the NHL's best defenseman when he won the Norris Trophy in 1976. Potvin would go on to capture the Trophy again in both 1978 and 1979.

10 Sittler completed his NHL career as a member of the Detroit Red Wings, suiting up for 61 games during the 1984-85 season.

11 On November 1st, 1959, Jacques Plante of the Montreal Canadiens was badly cut by a shot off the stick of the New York Rangers' Andy Bathgate. With the approval of Canadiens' management, Plante would wear the mask on a full-time basis, from that date on.

12 Raymond Bourque of the Boston Bruins won the Calder Trophy in 1980, Gretzky's first year in the NHL.

13 The Minnesota North Stars chose U.S. born Brian Lawton with the first pick of the 1983 Entry Draft.

14 Marcel Dionne, Dave Taylor and Charlie Simmer formed the potent "Triple Crown Line"

15 Darryl Sittler accumulated exactly 100 points on 41 goals and 59 assists during the 1975-76 regular season.

16 Hall of Fame member Doug Harvey would take over as captain of the Habs for the 1960-61 campaign. Harvey would captain the club for only the one season, moving on to become player/coach of the New York Rangers in 1961-62.

QUIZ 17 ANSWERS

1 Toe Blake won 500 games as coach of the Montreal Canadiens, Billy Reay was behind the bench for 516 wins for the Chicago Blackhawks and Al Arbour posted a record 739 victories while coach of the New York Islanders.

2 The Avalanche acquired Patrick Roy and Mike Keane from the Canadiens. Roy would lead the Colorado franchise to Stanley Cup Championships in both 1996 and 2001.

3 Billy Smith of the New York Islanders was notorious for hacking at the legs of opponents who dared to venture into his crease area, thus the nickname.

4 Phil Esposito of the Boston Bruins had a record 550 shots during the 1970-71 NHL season.

5 Charlie Conacher of the Toronto Maple Leafs was the NHL's leading point producer in both the 1933-34 and 1934-35 seasons.

6 Lanny McDonald's number 9 is the only number that has been retired by the Flames organization.

7 In 1979, Bryan Trottier became the first member of the Islanders to capture the Hart Trophy. He remains the only Islander to be voted the NHL's MVP.

8 Bernie Parent won a record 47 games for the Philadelphia Flyers during the 1973-74 season.

9 Jimmy Carson scored 55 times for the Los Angeles Kings during the 1987-88 season while Wayne Gretzky tallied 51 for the Edmonton Oilers in 1979-80. Carson and Gretzky were just 19 years of age when they accomplished this feat.

10 The Montreal Canadiens selected Gary Monahan from the St. Michael's Juveniles with the first pick of the 1963 Amateur Draft.

11 Pavel Bure scored 60 times in both the 1992-93 and 1993-94 seasons, to establish the Vancouver Canucks franchise record. Bure would later score 59 times for the Florida Panthers in 2000-01 to set the Panthers team record.

12 Lafleur played the final 59 games of his NHL career as a member of the Quebec Nordiques during the 1990-91 season.

13 The Ottawa Senators and the Tampa Bay Lightning became chartered members of the NHL in 1992. Both clubs would fail to make the Stanley Cup Playoffs in their initial season in the league.

14 Pembroke, Ontario-born Frank Nighbor was a dominant force in the NHL during the 1920s.

15 Born in Stockholm, Sweden, Pelle Lindbergh of the Philadelphia Flyers won the Vezina Trophy in 1985, becoming the first European to capture the prestigious award.

16 The Toronto Maple Leafs were the first NHL team to win the Stanley Cup three consecutive times. The Leafs won hockey's top prize in 1947, 1948 and 1949.

QUIZ 18 ANSWERS

1 Wayne Gretzky scored over 200 points in a season an astonishing four times as a member of the Edmonton Oilers. Gretzky had 215 points in the 1985-86 season, 212 in 1981-82, 208 in 1984-85 and 205 in 1983-84.

2 All of Ukranian descent, Bucyk, Horvath and Stasiuk were known as "The Uke Line".

3 On February 6th, 1986, Dave Andreychuk scored 5 times in an 8-6 Sabres victory over the Boston Bruins.

4 Peter Stastny of the Quebec Nordiques became the first NHL rookie to top 100 points in a season, when he scored 39 goals and added 70 assists for 109 points during the 1980-81 season.

5 Ken Dryden and Tony Esposito shared the goaltending duties for Team Canada 1972. Eddie Johnston saw no action in the series as Canada's third string goaltender.

6 Mark Messier captured the Hart Trophy in 1990, the last Oiler to be named the NHL's MVP.

7 Brent Gretzky played for the Tampa Bay Lightning from 1993 until 1995. He scored 1 goal and added 3 assists in his 13 career games.

8 Pierre Pilote of the Blackhawks was voted the NHL's premiere rearguard in 1963, 1964 and 1965.

9 Doug Gilmour scored 32 goals and added 95 assists for 127 points in the 1992-93 season to establish the Leafs record.

10 Mark Howe scored 41 goals and added 51 assists for 92 points to establish himself as the leading playoff point producer in the history of the WHA.

11 Shanahan began his NHL career as a member of the New Jersey Devils in the 1987-88 season.

12 Tony Esposito of the Chicago Blackhawks in 1970, Tom Barrasso of the Buffalo Sabres in 1984 , Ed Belfour of the Chicago Blackhawks in 1991 all won both the Calder and Vezina Trophys in the same season.

13 The Kings have retired #16 of Marcel Dionne, #18 of Dave Taylor, #30 of Rogie Vachon and #99 of Wayne Gretzky.

14 The Chicago Blackhawks have not won the Stanley Cup since the 1960-61 season.

15 In the 1942 Stanley Cup Final the Toronto Maple Leafs came all the way back from a 3-0 deficit to defeat the Detroit Red Wings 4 games to 3, claiming the Stanley Cup.

16 Reggie Leach of the Philadelphia Flyers scored a total of 15 times in his 10 game streak during the 1976 Stanley Cup Playoffs.

QUIZ 19 ANSWERS

1 Guy Lafleur of the Montreal Canadiens was the last member of an Original Six team to win the Art Ross Trophy when he recorded 132 points during the 1977-78 NHL regular season.

2 Tie Domi is considered to be one the NHL's premier fighters (pound for pound), in the league's history.

3 Roger Crozier of the Detroit Red Wings captured the Conn Smythe Trophy in 1966, despite the fact that his club lost in the Stanley Cup Final to the Montreal Canadiens.

4 Gil Stein became the last President of the NHL when he was named to the post in October of 1992.

5 The Detroit Red Wings finished first in the regular season seven consecutive seasons. The Wings led the NHL in points from 1948-49 until 1954-55.

6 Jeremy Roenick scored 46 goals and added 61 assists for 107 points for the Blackhawks during the 1993-94 season.

7 On April 11th, 1965, Norm Ullman of the Detroit Red Wings scored twice in 5 seconds, in a 4-2 victory over the Chicago Blackhawks.

8 Raymond Bourque's number 77 has been retired by both the Boston Bruins and the Colorado Avalanche.

9 Richard hit Bruin defender Hal Laycoe in the head with his stick and when referee Cliff Thompson attempted to intervene he too was struck by the furious Richard.

10 Hull played for the St. Catherine's Teepees of the OHA from 1955 until 1957, while Mikita played for the club from 1956 until 1959.

11 The Flyers' Schultz was given the nickname "The Hammer" for his fighting prowess during the 1970s. Schultz would accumulate almost 2300 penalty minutes in his 535 games in the NHL.

12 The Stars sent the Flames Corey Millen and junior star Jarome Iginla in exchange for the talented Nieuwendyk.

13 On April 11th, 1971, Bobby Orr of the Boston Bruins became the first NHL defenseman to score 3 times in a Stanley Cup Playoff game. Orr's hat trick led his Bruins to 5-2 victory over the Montreal Canadiens.

14 Doug Bentley, Max Bentley and Bill Mosienko formed the Hawks "Pony Line". The line would be the NHL's top scoring trio during the 1946-47 season.

15 Elmer Lach of the Montreal Canadiens scored 30 goals and added 31 assists for 61 points to win the Art Ross Trophy in 1948.

16 Gordie Howe of the Detroit Red Wings was 41 years of age when he totaled 103 points during the 1968-69 season.

QUIZ 20 ANSWERS

1 Paul Kariya of the Anaheim Mighty Ducks captured the Lady Byng Trophy in both 1996 and 1997.

2 Pavel Bure, who possessed incredible scoring ability, leading the NHL in goal scoring three times in his career.

3 Hap Day coached the Toronto Maple Leafs to five Stanley Cup Championships, while Hector "Toe" Blake led the Montreal Canadiens to eight titles and Scotty Bowman won a total of nine Stanley Cups with Montreal (5), Pittsburgh Penguins (1) and Detroit Red Wings (3).

4 Steve Yzerman scored 65 times during the 1988-89 season, to establish the Red Wing mark.

5 Reggie Leach of the Philadelphia Flyers first set the record when he scored 19 times in just 16 games during the 1976 Stanley Cup Playoffs. Jari Kurri of the Edmonton Oilers equaled the record in 18 games during the 1985 playoffs.

6 Wayne Gretzky of the Edmonton Oilers recorded 163 assists in the 1985-86 80 game schedule, for an average of 2.04 assists per game.

7 Daniel Alfredsson won the Calder Trophy in 1996, out-polling Eric Daze of the Chicago Blackhawks.

8 Barry Trotz was named coach of the Predators in 1998. As of 2006, Trotz remains the only coach in the history of the Nashville franchise.

9 Frank "Flash" Hollett of the Detroit Red Wings became the first NHL defenseman to reach 20 goals in a season. Hollett scored exactly 20 goals in 50 games during the 1944-45 NHL regular season.

10 In 1979-80, helmets became mandatory for players entering the NHL. Players already in the league, however, were exempt from the new ruling.

11 Mario Lemieux of the Pittsburgh Penguins was the last NHL'er to score 5 times in a playoff game. On April 25th, 1989, Lemieux's 5 goals led the Penguins to a 10-7 victory over the Philadelphia Flyers.

12 Frank Mahovlich was a fantastic skater who at times appeared to be lazy, thus infuriating the volatile Imlach.

13 Sergei Fedorov won both the Hart Trophy and Selke Trophy in 1994 while a member of the Detroit Red Wings.

14 Gordie Howe of the Detroit Red Wings was a first team selection 12 times, while Bobby Hull of the Chicago Blackhawks was named to the first team on 10 occasions.

15 Patrick Roy took part in 1029 NHL regular season games. Roy played 551 games for the Montreal Canadiens and 478 games as a member of the Colorado Avalanche.

16 Martin Havlat and Daniel Alfredsson both scored four goals for the Senators in a 10-4 victory over the Buffalo Sabres, on November 2nd, 2005.

QUIZ 21 ANSWERS

1 Nels Stewart scored 324 NHL goals during the 1920s and 1930s. Stewart played for the Montreal Maroons, Boston Bruins and New York Americans during his career.

2 Bobby Orr of the Boston Bruins was the first player to record 100 assists in a season. Wayne Gretzky accomplished the feat 8 times as a member of the Edmonton Oilers and 3 times as a member of the Los Angeles Kings, while Mario Lemieux of the Pittsburgh Penguins managed over 100 assists on a single occcassion.

3 Stan Mikita, Kenny Wharram and Doug Mohns were considered one of the NHL's most dominant trio of forwards during the late 1960s.

4 On May 4th, 1989, Alexander Mogilny signed with the NHL's Buffalo Sabres. Mogilny defected from the Soviet Union to join the team that selected him in the fourth round of the 1988 NHL Entry Draft.

5 Mike Bossy became the first Islander to top 50 goals in a season, when he fired 53 goals during the 1977-78 campaign.

6 The Flyers sent the Leafs' forward Rich Costello, a second round draft pick and future considerations in the Sittler deal.

7 Mike Gartner scored at least 30 goals in a season a record 17 times during his Hall of Fame career.

8 Peter Forsberg of the Colorado Avalanche was voted the NHL's MVP in 2003.

9 The Leafs' record for games played by an individual is held by George Armstrong. Armstrong played 1187 games in his NHL career, all as a member of the Leafs.

10 Iginla played for the Kamloops Blazers of the WHL from 1993 until 1996, accumulating 102 goals in his junior career.

11 Frank Calder was named the first President of the National Hockey League in 1917 and would remain in charge of the league until his death in 1943.

12 Wayne Gretzky won the Hart Trophy eight times while a member of the Edmonton Oilers and also captured the Trophy in 1989, his first season with the Los Angeles Kings. Mark Messier won the Hart Trophy in 1990 with the Oilers and again was named NHL MVP in 1992 as a member of the New York Rangers.

13 Gary Unger was the first NHLer to play 900 straight games. Unger would go onto play in a then record 914 consecutive games, spanning over a decade.

14 The 1974-75 Washington Capitals set the NHL record for futility. The Capitals won just 8 times and tied 5 others while losing 67 games in the 80 game schedule.

15 Mike Richter of the New York Rangers won MVP honors in the 1994 NHL All-Star game.

16 Tom Johnson was behind the Bruin bench for the club's 1972 Stanley Cup victory.

QUIZ 22 ANSWERS

1 Rookie Gary Suter of the Calgary Flames recorded six assists in a 9-3 victory over the Edmonton Oilers on April 4th, 1986.

2 On February 1st, 1976, Gilbert Perreault scored twice and added five assists for seven points in a 9-5 Sabres win over the California Golden Seals.

3 Harvey "Busher" Jackson was elected to the Hall of Fame in 1971. Smythe was appalled by Jackson's hard living lifestyle.

4 The Leafs' Gordie Drillon led the NHL with 26 goals and 26 assists for 52 points in the 1937-38 regular season.

5 Bobby Orr of the Boston Bruins won both the Hart and Smythe Trophys in 1970 and again in 1972. Guy Lafleur of the Montreal Canadiens won both Trophys in 1977 and Wayne Gretzky of the Edmonton Oilers won the pair in 1985.

6 On June 2nd, 1993, Eric Desjardins of the Montreal Canadiens became the first NHL defenseman to score 3 times in a Stanley Cup Finals game, scoring all 3 of the Habs goals in a 3-2 victory over the Los Angeles Kings.

7 Jari Kurri of the Edmonton Oilers scored 52 times during the 1983-84 season.

8 Sergei Makarov of the Calgary Flames was 31 years of age when he captured the Calder Trophy in 1990.

9   Eddie Shack scored 239 goals during his NHL career and entertained millions of fans with his robust style of play.

10   Brian Leetch of the New York Rangers scored 22 goals and added 80 assists for 102 points during the 1991-92 regular season.

11   Dryden played at Cornell University from 1966 until 1969, while Nieuwendyk starred at the school from 1984 until 1987.

12   On January 30th, 1973, Jim Harrison of the Alberta Oilers set the WHA record of ten points in a game. Harrison scored four times and added six assists in establishing the record.

13   The Kansas City Scouts and the Washington Capitals joined the National Hockey League in 1974.

14   Doug Gilmour became the only member of the Leafs to be voted the NHL's best defensive forward, winning the Selke Trophy in 1993.

15   Mark Messier scored 14 times in the Stanley Cup Playoffs, while his team was a man short.

16   Larry Murphy set the Los Angeles Kings record of 76 points during the 1980-81 season and established the Washington Capitals record of 81 points during the 1986-87 NHL campaign.

QUIZ 23 ANSWERS

1 The Leafs chose Al Iafrate with the 4th overall selection of the 1984 NHL Entry Draft. Iafrate was a offensive force early in his career but was considered rather reckless defensively.

2 On March 7th, 1975, Guy Lafleur became the first Hab to reach 100 points in a season. Lafleur would finish the 1974-75 schedule with a then club record 119 points.

3 The Thrashers chose Patrik Stefan with the first overall selection of the 1999 NHL Entry Draft.

4 Leonard "Red" Kelly was the first coach of the Los Angeles Kings. Kelly was behind the Kings bench for both the 1967-68 and 1968-69 seasons.

5 Boucher and the Cook brothers were known as the "Bread Line". They would be the dominant trio in the NHL throughout the 1930s.

6 On March 23rd, 1944, Maurice Richard scored all five of the Montreal Canadiens goals as the Habs defeated the Toronto Maple Leafs 5-1.

7 Gordie Howe appeared in 23 NHL All-Star games, 22 as a member of the Detroit Red Wings and one as a member of the Hartford Whalers.

8 Marian Hossa of the Ottawa Senators had his stick accidentally strike Berard as he followed through with his shot. It was thought that Berard's career had come to an end but miraculously he returned to the National Hockey League in 2001 as a member of the New York Rangers.

9 Derek Sanderson's centering pass from behind the St. Louis Blues net enabled Orr to score the 1970 Stanley Cup winning goal. His shot beat Glenn Hall to give the Bruins a four game sweep of the Blues.

10 Johnny Bower and Terry Sawchuk of the Toronto Maple Leafs, in 1964-65.

11 Jean Ratelle won the Lady Byng Trophy as the NHL's most gentlemanly player in 1976. Ratelle was traded to the Boston Bruins from the New York Rangers during the 1975-76 season.

12 Chris Chelios won the James Norris Trophy in 1989, outdistancing runner-up Paul Coffey of the Pittsburgh Penguins.

13 Claire Alexander quit his job as a milkman in Orillia, Ontario, to play pro hockey. He joined the Leafs for the 1974-75 season and played three seasons with the team before being traded to the Vancouver Canucks on January 29th, 1978.

14 Phil Esposito of the Boston Bruins led the NHL in goal scoring from the 1969-70 season until the 1974-75 season, an NHL record six seasons in a row.

15 Wayne Gretzky in 1983, Mario Lemieux in 1990, Vincent Damphousse in 1991, Mike Gartner in 1993 and Dany Heatley in 2003, all scored 4 times in the NHL All-Star game.

16 Dale Hawerchuk potted 53 goals for the Jets during the 1984-85 regular season.

QUIZ 24 ANSWERS

1 The Flyers sent Peter Forsberg, Ron Hextall, Mike Ricci, Kerry Huffman, Steve Duchesne, a first round draft choice and $15,000,000 in cash to the Nordiques for Lindros' services.

2 Kent Douglas of the Toronto Maple Leafs became the first defenseman to capture the Calder Trophy when he won the award in 1963.

3 Ken Dryden of the Montreal Canadiens won 258 times while losing just 57 games during his Hall of Fame career.

4 Raymond Bourque took off his sweater number 7 and handed it to Esposito. Bourque then revealed his new number, 77, the number he would wear the rest of his NHL career.

5 On November 13th, 1934, defenseman Ralph "Scotty" Bowman of the St. Louis Eagles scored the first penalty shot goal in NHL history. Bowman beat Montreal Maroons goaltender Alec Connell with his historic shot.

6 Although considered to be one of hockey's greatest stars of all time, Richard won only the 1947 Hart Memorial Trophy as the NHL's most valuable player.

7 Gainey played for the Peterborough Petes of the OJMHL from 1971 until 1973.

8 Adam Oates finished runner up in Lady Byng voting from 1993 until 1996. Wayne Gretzky also finished second four consecutive years and won the Trophy fives times during his career.

9 Finland's Teemu Selanne has been a scoring sensation since he entered the NHL in 1992.

10 Dave Keon took over as the Leafs captain to begin the 1971-72 schedule. Keon would remain the club's captain until the end of the 1974-75 season.

11 The Hobey Baker Award has been awarded to the outstanding player in the NCAA, since 1981.

12 Bobby Orr played for the Oshawa Generals of the OHA from 1963 until 1966. Orr recorded 257 points in his 159 regular season games with the Generals.

13 The Atlanta Thrashers chose Ilya Kovalchuk first overall in the 2001 Entry Draft and the Washington Capitals took Alexander Ovechkin with the first selection of the 2004 Entry Draft.

14 In the 1985-86 season, Tim Kerr of the Philadelphia Flyers scored a record 34 times while his Flyers enjoyed a man advantage.

15 Lanny McDonald scored a Flames club record 66 goals during the 1982-83 regular season.

16 Bobby Orr won the Norris Trophy a record eight times, while Doug Harvey won it seven times and Raymond Bourque captured the honor five times.

QUIZ 25 ANSWERS

1 The Detroit Red Wings won the Stanley Cup in both 1997 and 1998.

2 Terry Sawchuk won 447 NHL games during his Hall of Fame career.

3 Doug Weight scored 25 goals and added 79 assists for 104 points during the 1995-96 regular season.

4 Inge Hammarstrom, one of the first Swedish-born players in the NHL. He played a timid yet productive game for the Leafs, recording three 20 goal seasons with the team.

5 Gretzky played eight games for the WHA's Indianapolis Racers in the 1978-79 season. Gretzky would be traded to the Edmonton Oilers that season and wind up with 110 points in his only season in the league.

6 Glenn Hall of the St. Louis Blues was 37 years of age when he won the Conn Smythe Trophy in 1968.

7 On February 3rd, 1982, Grant Mulvey of the Blackhawks scored 5 times in a 9-5 victory versus the St. Louis Blues.

8 "The Gold Dust Twins", Gus Mortson and Jimmy Thomson, each won four Stanley Cup rings as members of the Leafs, in the late 1940s and early 1950s.

9 Howie Morenz of the Montreal Canadiens was the first player to capture the Hart Trophy in back to back seasons. Morenz won the NHL's MVP honors in 1931 and again in 1932.

10 The Philadelphia Quakers played only one season in the NHL. In the 1930-31 season, the Quakers managed only 4 victories in 44 contests and quickly disappeared from the league.

11 Larry Murphy of the Los Angeles Kings scored 16 goals and added 60 assists for 76 points in 1980-81, his rookie year.

12 On December 30th, 1981, Gretzky scored his 50th goal of the season in just his 39th game. Gretzky would score 5 times in the game, with his 50th of the season scored into an empty net in a 7-5 Oiler victory over the Philadelphia Flyers.

13 Martin Brodeur in 1994 and Scott Gomez in 2000 are the only Devils to take home NHL rookie of the year honors.

14 The Calgary Cowboys were members of the WHA's Canadian Division in 1975-76 and the league's Western Division in 1976-77.

15 Chris Pronger of the St. Louis Blues won both the Hart Trophy and Norris Trophy in 2000.

16 The number 2 has been retired by the Buffalo Sabres to honor Tim Horton, by the Montreal Canadiens to honor Doug Harvey and the St. Louis Blues to honor Al MacInnis.

QUIZ 26 ANSWERS

1 Dickie Moore wore the number 12 for the Canadiens from 1951 until 1963 while Yvan Cournoyer wore the jersey from 1963-64 until his retirement at the conclusion of the 1979 season.

2 Frank Brimsek was an outstanding NHL netminder throughout the 1940s, leading the league in shutouts twice during his Hall of Fame career.

3 Thornton played for the Sault Ste. Marie Greyhounds of the OHL from 1995 until 1997. He was claimed first overall in the 1997 NHL Entry Draft by the Boston Bruins.

4 Patrick Roy won the Conn Smythe Trophy as a member of the Montreal Canadiens in 1986 and 1993. Roy won the award a third time as a member of the Colorado Avalanche in 2001.

5 Bobby Hull of the Chicago Blackhawks became the first player in NHL history to exceed 50 goals in a season when he scored 54 times during the 1965-66 schedule.

6 Mike Bossy and Wayne Gretzky both scored 50 or more goals in an NHL season 9 times during their fabulous careers.

7 With the second and third overall picks of the 1999 NHL Entry Draft, the Vancouver Canucks chose twins Daniel and Henrik Sedin.

8 Terry Sawchuk began his NHL career with the Detroit Red Wings in 1949-50 and finished his career as a member of the New York Rangers in 1969-70.

9 In an effort to reduce tie games, the NHL introduced regular season sudden-death overtime to begin the 1983-84 season.

10 Bob Plager played 644 games in the NHL while brothers Barclay and Bill played 614 and 263 NHL games respectively.

11 Bryan Trottier won the Art Ross Trophy in the 1978-79 season. Trottier scored 47 goals and added 87 assists for 134 points, to claim the award.

12 Carl Voss of the Detroit Red Wings was the first recipient of the Calder Trophy.

13 The Montreal Canadiens and the Boston Bruins faced each other a record eight times in the Stanley Cup Finals. Incredibly, the Canadiens captured the Cup on all eight occasions.

14 On November 9th, 2005, Erik Cole of the Carolina Hurricanes was awarded two penalty shots. Cole went one for two on his attempts in a 5-3 Hurricanes victory over the Buffalo Sabres.

15 Doug Jarvis played in 964 consecutive games to establish the NHL record. Jarvis began his streak on October 8th, 1975, as a member of the Montreal Canadiens and ended his run on October 10th, 1987, while a member of the Hartford Whalers.

16 Bobby Orr of the Boston Bruins set the NHL single season assist record in 1970-71 when he registered 102 helpers.

1 In 2004, Martin St. Louis of the Tampa Bay Lightning won the Art Ross Trophy as the NHL's leading scorer, the Hart Trophy as MVP and the Lester B. Pearson Award as the league's MVP as voted by the NHLPA.

2 Although the law let Don Murdoch of the New York Rangers off with a fine, the NHL saw fit to suspend him for one year. Although the suspension was halved on appeal, Murdoch's career was virtually destroyed.

3 Bernie Parent of the Philadelphia Flyers and Tony Esposito of the Chicago Blackhawks tied for the Vezina Trophy in 1974. Both teams allowed only 164 goals apiece during the regular season.

4 Bernie Federko scored 352 goals and added 721 assists for 1073 points to establish the Blues franchise record.

5 Montreal hosted the NHL Entry Draft at various locations from 1963 until 1984. The first Draft held outside of Montreal took place at the Toronto Convention Centre in 1985.

6 Vladimir Krutov, Igor Larionov and Sergei Makarov formed the Soviet Union's devastating "KLM" line. All three would join NHL teams in 1989-90.

7 Gus Bodnar assisted on all 3 of Mosienko's goals thus establishing the NHL record for the fastest 3 assists in a single game by an individual.

8 Henri Richard was known as "The Pocket Rocket". Although somewhat overshadowed by brother Maurice, Henri would put up some very impressive numbers during his Hall of Fame career.

9 Lemieux played for the Laval Voisins of the QMJHL from 1981 until 1984. Lemieux accumulated an amazing 562 points in just 200 games as a member of the Voisins.

10 On April 9th, 1968, Wayne Connelly of the Minnesota North Stars beat Los Angeles Kings netminder Terry Sawchuk for the NHL's first penalty shot goal in Stanley Cup Playoff history.

11 Goaltender George Hainsworth captained the Montreal Canadiens in 1932-33.

12 Windsor, Ontario native Brad Smith was known as "Motor City Smitty". Though possessing little natural talent, Smith's honest effort endeared him with fans wherever he played.

13 Jack Adams was a center on the Stanley Cup Champion 1917-18 Toronto Arenas and the 1926-27 Chicago Blackhawks. Adams led the Detroit Red Wings to three Stanley Cups as coach and general manager during the 1930s and 1940s.

14 Lorne Worsley captured the Calder Trophy in 1953 as a member of the New York Rangers yet Johnny Bower played all 70 games for the Rangers the following season.

15 On February 7th, 1976, Darryl Sittler of the Toronto Maple Leafs scored 6 goals and added 4 assists for 10 points in a 11-4 victory over the Boston Bruins.

16 The San Jose Sharks lost an NHL record 71 games during the 1992-93 season. The Sharks won only 11 times in the 84 game schedule.

QUIZ 28 ANSWERS

1 Gordie Howe of the Detroit Red Wings scored 9 goals and added 11 assists for 20 points during the 1955 Stanley Cup Playoffs.

2 Hakan Loob of the Calgary Flames scored 50 times during the 1988-89 campaign.

3 Ken Daneyko played his entire NHL career with the Devils. Daneyko played a total of 1283 regular season games from 1983 until 2003 with New Jersey.

4 Maurice "Rocket" Richard of the Montreal Canadiens scored goal number 500 of his NHL career on October 19th, 1957, against Glenn Hall of the Chicago Blackhawks.

5 Billy Taylor of the Detroit Red Wings recorded 7 assists in a game on March 16th, 1947, against the Chicago Blackhawks.

6 Walter "Turk" Broda captured the Vezina Trophy in 1941 with a goals against average of 2.06.

7 Eric Staal played for the Peterborough Petes of the OHL from 2000 until 2003. Staal was chosen 2nd overall in the 2003 NHL Entry Draft by the Carolina Hurricanes.

8 Phil Housley of the Buffalo Sabres was just 20 years of age when he scored 31 goals in the 1983-84 season.

9 Joe Nieuwendyk was voted the MVP of the 1999 Stanley Cup Playoffs, leading the Stars to Cup victory over the Buffalo Sabres.

10 The Columbus Blue Jackets and the Minnesota Wild joined the National Hockey League in 2000.

11 Bobby Orr of the Boston Bruins won the Calder Trophy in 1967 and would go on to capture the Hart Trophy in 1970, 1971 and 1972.

12 The St. Louis Blues' Brett Hull scored 86 times in 1990-91, 72 times in 1989-90 and 70 times in 1991-92.

13 The Bruins won the Stanley Cup in 1929, 1939, 1942, 1970 and 1972 for a total of five Championships.

14 Terry Crisp coached the Lightning from 1992 until 1998.

15 Defenseman Lionel Conacher of the Chicago Blackhawks and right winger Charlie Conacher of the Toronto Maple Leafs were chosen to the NHL's First All-Star Team in 1933-34.

16 Goaltender Dominik Hasek of the Buffalo Sabres won the Hart Trophy in 1997 and again in 1998.

QUIZ 29 ANSWERS

1 The Senators chose Bryan Berard from the Detroit Jr. Red Wings in 1995 and selected Prince Albert Raiders' Chris Phillips in 1996.

2 Terry Sawchuk shut out the opponent 103 times in his 972 NHL regular season games.

3 Gordie Howe played 26 seasons in the NHL while Mark Messier retired in 2005 having played 25 years in the league.

4 The Philadelphia Flyers created mayhem on their way to back to back Stanley Cup Championships in 1974 and 1975.

5 On February 12th, 1947, Aubrey "Dit" Clapper of the Boston Bruins played his final NHL game and was inducted into hockey's hallowed hall at game's end. The Bruins also retired Clapper's jersey number 5 that same night.

6 Harry Neale issued this hilarious quote while coach of a struggling Vancouver Canucks.

7 Barclay Plager was a member of the Blues from 1967 until 1977, while brother Bob suited up for the club from 1967 until 1978 and brother Bill played for the team from 1968 until 1972.

8 Mike Bossy played his entire NHL career with the Islanders, scoring 573 goals in just 752 games with the team.

9 Dany Heatley of the Atlanta Thrashers scored 4 times in the 2003 NHL All-Star game.

10 In the 1987-88 NHL season, Craig Simpson scored 13 goals for the Pittsburgh Penguins before being traded to the Edmonton Oilers. Simpson would tally 43 more goals with the Oilers for a season total of 56.

11 Eric Lindros was chosen first overall by the Quebec Nordiques in the 1991 NHL Entry Draft.

12 The Sabres previously retired the number 2 of Tim Horton, the number 7 of Richard Martin, the number 11 of Gilbert Perreault and the number 14 of Rene Robert.

13 Paul Coffey of the Edmonton Oilers scored 12 times during the 1985 Stanley Cup Playoffs.

14 Gartner began his NHL career as a Washington Capital in 1979. He would go on to play for the Minnesota North Stars, New York Rangers and Toronto Maple Leafs before ending his stint in the NHL with the Phoenix Coyotes in 1998.

15 Scotty Bowman was behind the bench for 223 Playoff victories while coaching the St. Louis Blues, Montreal Canadiens, Buffalo Sabres, Pittsburgh Penguins and Detroit Red Wings.

16 The Leafs sent Wendel Clark, Sylvain Lefebvre and Landon Wilson to the Nordiques in a trade that shocked the hockey world.

QUIZ 30 ANSWERS

1 Mickey Redmond scored 52 times for the Wings during the 1973-74 regular season.

2 Derek Sanderson, who won NHL rookie of the year honors in 1968 as a member of the Boston Bruins. Sanderson possessed a nasty streak that often infuriated his opponents.

3 John A. Ziegler Jr. took over as NHL President in 1977. He would head the league until 1992.

4 Cam Neely of the Boston Bruins scored 50 goals in just 49 games during the 1993-94 season.

5 Cheecho played for the Belleville Bulls of the OHL from 1997 until 2000.

6 Richard's Montral Canadien teammate Bernie Geoffrion was the second NHLer to score 50 times in a season. Geoffrion scored his 50th goal of the 1960-61 season on March 16th, 1961 against Cesare Maniago of the Toronto Maple Leafs.

7 Roger Neilson coached the expansion Panthers in 1993-94, leading them to an impressive 33 wins in their inaugural season in the NHL.

8 The Leafs' Dave Keon won the Lady Byng Trophy in both 1962 and 1963.

9 Gilbert Perreault played 1191 NHL games for the Sabres and Craig Ramsay participated in 1070 games with the team.

10 Theo Fleury recorded exactly 100 points during the 1992-93 NHL regular season.

11 Pat Stapleton, Paul Henderson and Frank Mahovlich played on both the National Hockey League's 1972 team and the World Hockey Association's 1974 team.

12 Mats Sundin of the Toronto Maple Leafs failed to score on the Philadelphia Flyers' John Vanbiesbrouck on April 22nd, 1999 and was successful against the Buffalo Sabres' Dominik Hasek on May 29th, 1999.

13 Bobby Hull of the Chicago Blackhawks won the Hart Trophy in 1965 and 1966. Bobby's son Brett captured the award in 1991 while a member of the St. Louis Blues.

14 Scotty Bowman was behind the bench for 2141 games during his 30 years as a coach in the National Hockey League.

15 Wayne Gretzky won the Lady Byng Trophy in 1999.

16 Howie Morenz of the Montreal Canadiens scored 33 goals and added 18 assists for 51 points during the 1927-28 season.

QUIZ 31 ANSWERS

1 Gilles Gilbert of the Boston Bruins won 17 straight games during the 1975-76 season.

2 The Montreal Canadiens chose Guy Lafleur with the first pick in 1971 and the Detroit Red Wings selected Marcel Dionne second overall.

3 John Bucyk scored 545 of his 556 NHL goals while a member of the Bruins.

4 Bryan "Bugsy" Watson accumulated a then record 2212 penalty minutes in a NHL career that spanned 16 NHL seasons.

5 Mike Bossy of the New York Islanders scored 53 times during the 1977-78 season while Joe Nieuwendyk of the Calgary Flames tallied 51 in 1987-88. Teemu Selanne of the Winnipeg Jets notched an incredible 76 goals in 1992-93 and Alexander Ovechkin of the Washington Capitals scored 52 goals during the 2005-06 regular season.

6 Terry Sawchuk in 1951, Glenn Hall in 1956 and Roger Crozier in 1965 all won NHL rookie of the year honors.

7 Best known as a member of the Toronto Maple Leafs, Borje Salming was inducted into the Hockey Hall of Fame in 1996.

8 Chris Chelios was selected to the NHL's First All-Star Team in 1995-96.

9 On October 30th, 1943, Gus Bodnar of the Toronto Maple Leafs set the NHL record by scoring just 15 seconds into his NHL debut, in a 5-2 victory over the New York Rangers.

10 Bernie Parent left the Toronto Maple Leafs to join the Blazers for the inaugural WHA season.

11 Rod Langway of the Capitals won the Norris Trophy in both 1983 and 1984.

12 Howie Meeker of the Toronto Maple Leafs took home NHL rookie of the year honors in 1947.

13 Patrik Sundstrom of the New Jersey Devils scored 3 goals and added 5 assists for 8 points, on April 22, 1988 and Mario Lemieux of the Pittsburgh Penguins had 8 points on 5 goals and 3 assists on April 25th, 1989.

14 The Bruins called the Boston Garden home for over 70 years.

15 Maurice Richard leads all Canadiens with 544 goals followed by Guy Lafleur with 518 and Jean Beliveau with 507.

16 Best known as a Detroit Red Wing, Sid Abel was inducted into the Hockey Hall of Fame in 1969.

QUIZ 32 ANSWERS

1 The Americans beat Finland 4-2 in their last game of the 1980 Winter Olympics in Lake Placid, New York to clinch the gold medal.

2 Babe Pratt won the Hart Trophy in 1944 and in 1955 Ted Kennedy would become the last Leaf to capture the award.

3 Scott Young wrote many books on hockey. Young was inducted into the Hockey Hall of Fame as a media honoree in 1988.

4 Gordie Howe of the Detroit Red Wings won the Art Ross trophy as the NHL's top scorer in 1950-51, 1951-52, 1952-53, 1953-54 and 1956-57 for a total of five in the decade.

5 Jari Kurri of the Edmonton Oilers recorded 4 hat tricks in the 1985 Stanley Cup Playoffs.

6 Yvan Cournoyer was lightning quick. Cournoyer would play all 968 games of his NHL career as a member of the Montreal Canadiens.

7 Jean Beliveau of the Montreal Canadiens wore the number 4 in the 1968 NHL All-Star game due to the fact that he had more seniority in the league.

8 The Challenge Cup replaced the NHL All-Star game in 1979. This one time only series was captured by the Soviets.

9   Rod Gilbert scored 406 goals and added 615 assists for 1021 points in his career with the Rangers.

10   From 1981-82 until 1985-86, five years in a row, the Edmonton Oilers scored 400 or more goals in a season.

11   Charlie Conacher was gifted goal scorer throughout the 1930s. Conacher would score 200 of his 225 NHL goals while a member of the Toronto Maple Leafs.

12   On November 12th, 1942, Bep Guidolin, just 16 years of age, suited up for the Boston Bruins, becoming the youngest player to appear in an NHL game.

13   Paul Coffey of the Edmonton Oilers scored 48 goals during the 1985-86 schedule to establish the NHL record.

14   Ron Francis won the Selke Trophy out-polling Esa Tikkanen of the St. Louis Blues in voting for the award.

15   Martin St. Louis won the Hart Trophy in 2003-04, leading the Lightning to the Stanley Cup title.

16   Robinson played for the Los Angeles Kings from 1989-90 until his retirement at the conclusion of the 1991-92 schedule.

QUIZ 33 ANSWERS

1 Gino Odjick was penalized 2127 minutes in just 444 games as a member of the Canucks.

2 Joe Mullen of the Pittsburgh Penguins became the first American to score 500 NHL goals when he fired number 500 on February 7th, 1995. Mullen would conclude his career with 502 NHL goals.

3 Howie Morenz of the Montreal Canadiens was without doubt the finest player in the National Hockey League during the 1920s.

4 Dennis Maruk scored 60 times for the Capitals during the 1981-82 season to establish the record.

5 Although the New York Rangers failed to make the Stanley Cup Playoffs in 1958-59, Andy Bathgate was deemed to be the NHL's most valuable player.

6 Denis Potvin was the first overall selection in the 1973 Entry Draft and would capture the Calder Trophy for 1973-74. Bryan Berard was the first player taken in the 1995 Entry Draft and would go on to cop NHL rookie of the year honors for 1996-97.

7 In 1975, Marcel Dionne became the last Red Wing to win the Lady Byng Trophy.

8 Wayne Gretzky scored his 500th NHL goal in just his 575th NHL game while Mario Lemieux took 605 games to reach the mark. Mike Bossy notched number 500 in his 647th game and Brett Hull reached the milestone in game 693 of his NHL career.

9 In 2000-01, Dave King became the first coach of the Blue Jackets.

10 Bobby Hull scored 604 goals for the Hawks and Stan Mikita scored all 541 of his NHL career goals while a member of the team.

11 Although both Dennis Murphy and Gary Davidson possessed little hockey knowledge their astute business sense would see the league survive for seven eventful seasons.

12 Gilbert Perreault, Richard Martin and Rene Robert led the Sabres to their first Stanley Cup Final in 1975.

13 Dave Keon of the Toronto Maple Leafs scored twice while his team was a man short on April 18th, 1963, in a 3-1 Leaf victory over the Detroit Red Wings.

14 Rob Blake played a punishing brand of hockey in capturing the 1998 Norris Trophy.

15 Grant Fuhr of the Edmonton Oilers was just 19 years of age when he took part in the 1982 NHL All-Star game.

16 Doug Gilmour was known as a fierce competitor throughout the 1474 games of his NHL career.

1 Vic Howe played for the New York Rangers in the early 1950s, scoring 3 goals and adding 4 assists in his short stay in the NHL.

2 The Montreal Canadiens won five Stanley Cups in a row from 1956 until 1960, they also won four straight titles from 1976 to 1979. The New York Islanders were the last team to win four consecutive Cups when they took home Lord Stanley's jug from 1980 until 1983.

3 Ernie Wakely recorded 16 shutouts with five different teams to establish the WHA record.

4 Mike Keenan was behind the bench when the Rangers last won the Stanley Cup in 1994.

5 Glen Sather called Wayne Gretzky "Brinks" after "The Great One" signed a lucrative contract with the Edmonton Oilers.

6 In what turned out to be an extremely one sided trade the Sabres picked up Dominik Hasek from the Hawks.

7 Gordie Howe appeared in his first All-Star game in 1948 and would make his final appearance in the 1980 game in Detroit.

8 Goalies Martin Brodeur of the New Jersey Devils, Curtis Joseph of the Toronto Maple Leafs and Ed Belfour of the Dallas Stars represented Canada at the 2002 Winter Olympic Games in Salt Lake City, Utah.

9 Pierre Larouche scored 53 times for the Pittsburgh Penguins in the 1975-76 season and tallied 50 goals in 1979-80 for the Montreal Canadiens.

10 Gerry Cheevers of the Boston Bruins went undefeated in 32 straight games during the 1971-72 NHL regular season.

11 The first NHL All-Star game was held as benefit for "Ace" Bailey of the Toronto Maple Leafs. Bailey's career ended on December 12th, 1933, when he suffered a serious head injury at the hands of the Boston Bruin, Eddie Shore.

12 Kevin Lowe would play 1037 of his 1254 career NHL games with the Oilers.

13 Joe Malone of the Montreal Canadiens scored 44 times in just 20 games during the 1917-18 season.

14 Lafontaine played the final 67 games of his NHL career with the New York Rangers in 1997-98.

15 Bernie Geoffrion of the Montreal Canadiens won the Calder Trophy in 1952 and would take home the Hart Trophy in 1961.

16 Colorado Avalanche goaltender Patrick Roy surrendered Yzerman's, Mullen's and Shanahan's 500th goals of their NHL careers.

QUIZ 35 ANSWERS

1 On December 23rd, 1978, Bryan Trottier scored 5 goals and added 3 assists for 8 points, establishing the Islanders record.

2 The Cincinnati Stingers were members of the World Hockey Association from 1975 until 1979.

3 Wayne Gretzky scored 40 or more goals in a season 12 times in his NHL career while both Marcel Dionne and Mario Lemieux accomplished the feat 10 times.

4 Jacques Laperriere of the Montreal Canadiens won rookie of the year honors in 1964, becoming only the second defenseman in NHL history to win the Calder Trophy.

5 The Maple Leafs were known as the Toronto St. Patricks from 1919-20 until partway into the 1926-27 NHL schedule.

6 Glen Sather was both coach and general manager of the Oilers for their Stanley Cup victories in 1984, 1985, 1987 and 1988.

7 Brad Park finished second in Norris Trophy voting six times in his career. Park finished second to Bobby Orr four times and was runner-up to Denis Potvin on two occasions. Raymond Bourque was also bridesmaid in Norris Trophy voting six times, however he took home the award five times during his NHL career.

8 Bob "Battleship" Kelly was a hard-nosed player who was also a capable offensive force as he scored 154 goals in 12 seasons in the National Hockey League.

9 In 1967, Jim Pappin of the Leafs scored 7 goals and added 8 assists for 15 points to lead the league in playoff scoring.

10 In 1986, the Montreal Canadiens defeated the Calgary Flames 4 games to 1 in the Stanley Cup Final and the Flames got their revenge by beating the Canadiens 4 games to 2 in 1989.

11 Bob Gainey of the Montreal Canadiens impressed Tikhonov with his outstanding defensive abilities and his flashes of offensive brilliance.

12 Paul Coffey of the Edmonton Oilers had 37 points in the 1985 Stanley Cup Playoffs, Brian Leetch of the New York Rangers had 34 in 1994 and Al MacInnis of the Calgary Flames recorded 31 points in 1989.

13 The legendary Foster Hewitt began broadcasting Toronto Maple Leafs games from the old Mutual Street Arena in the 1920s. His signature "He shoots, he scores" is arguably the most famous phrase in all of sport.

14 Richard Martin of the Buffalo Sabres scored 44 times during the 1971-72 season.

15 Bobby Hull, Ulf Nilsson and Anders Hedberg formed the most exciting forward line in the short history of the WHA.

16 From February 24th, 1968 until December 21st, 1979 Garry Unger never missed an NHL game, a span of 914 straight games.

QUIZ 36 ANSWERS

1 Canada, Finland, Sweden, Czechoslovakia, the USSR and the United States took part in the first Canada Cup in 1976.

2 Wayne Gretzky scored at least 3 goals in a game 50 times in his career. Gretzky scored 3 goals in a game 37 times, 4 goals in a game on 9 occasions and 4 times notched 5 goals in a single NHL game.

3 Tommy Gorman coached the Chicago Blackhawks to the 1934 Stanley Cup and was behind the bench for the Montreal Maroon's Cup victory in 1935.

4 Grant Fuhr of the Edmonton Oilers recorded 14 assists in the 1983-84 regular season.

5 The Atlanta Flames and the New York Islanders joined the NHL in 1972-73. Both the Flames and Islanders failed to qualify for the Stanley Cup Playoffs in their first season in the NHL.

6 Wayne "Swoop" Carleton, began his NHL career as a member of the Toronto Maple Leafs and would play parts of seven seasons in the league, before departing for the rebel WHA.

7 Raymond Bourque of the Boston Bruins won the Calder Trophy and was selected to the NHL's First All-Star Team, on defense, in 1979-80.

8 Jacques Plante of the Montreal Canadiens had the NHL's best goals against average five years in succession, from 1956 until 1960 inclusive.

9 Bobby Clarke played all of his 1144 NHL games with the Flyers, in a Hall of Fame career that spanned 15 seasons.

10 Roy played for the Granby Bisons of the QMJHL from 1982 until 1985.

11 Great Britain won the Olympic Gold Medal in hockey at the Winter Olympic games in Garmisch-Partenkirchen, Germany in 1936. All but one of the members of the British team were of British origin but had been raised and trained in Canada. Carl Erhardt was the only true Englishman on the team.

12 The Montreal Canadiens' Maurice "Rocket" Richard scored 50 times in the 1944-45 regular season , Bernie Geoffrion of the Canadiens had 50 goals during the 1960-61 campaign and Bobby Hull scored 50 goals for the first time in his career in the 1961-62 season.

13 Rick Nash of the Columbus Blue Jackets, Jarome Iginla of the Calgary Flames and Ilya Kovalchuk of the Atlanta Thrashers each scored 41 goals to top the NHL in 2003-04.

14 Paul Kariya became the first Duck to score 50 goals when he notched exactly 50 during the 1995-96 NHL schedule.

15 Goaltender, Turk Broda of the Toronto Maple Leafs appeared in 101 Stanley Cup Playoff games in his NHL career. Broda would backstop the Leafs to 5 Stanley Cup titles during the 1940s and 1950s.

16 The 1992-93 Pittsburgh Penguins won 17 straight games from March 9th, 1993 until April 10th, 1993.

QUIZ 37 ANSWERS

1 Born in Riverton, Manitoba, Reggie Leach helped the Flyers to a Stanley Cup Championship in 1975.

2 Mats Naslund scored 43 goals and added 67 assists for 110 points during the 1985-86 regular season.

3 Harvey's Montreal Canadiens teammate Tom Johnson won the Norris Trophy in 1959.

4 The Rangers' Brian Leetch won the Calder Trophy in 1989, defeating runner-up Trevor Linden of the Vancouver Canucks in voting for the award.

5 Mark Messier announced his retirement from the NHL's New York Rangers in 2005. Messier began his professional hockey career with the WHA's Indianapolis Racers in 1979.

6 On March 20th, 1971, Ken Dryden's Montreal Canadiens defeated Dave Dryden's Buffalo Sabres 5-2 at the Montreal Forum.

7 The very cerebral Wayne Gretzky describing his uncanny ability to know where the play is going.

8 Jean Beliveau, Dickie Moore and Bernie Geoffrion would all win the Art Ross Trophy as the NHL's leading scorer at least once during illustrious careers.

9 Jean Ratelle recorded 109 points for the New York Rangers in 1971-72 and would tally 105 points while a member of the 1975-76 Boston Bruins.

10 Al Arbour was coach of the New York Islanders for 1499 regular season games and Billy Reay was behind the bench for 1012 games with the Chicago Blackhawks.

11 Martin Brodeur of the New Jersey Devils registered 7 shutouts during the 2003 Stanley Cup Playoffs.

12 The San Diego Mariners were members of the WHA from 1974 until 1977.

13 Red Berenson of the St. Louis Blues scored 6 times on November 7th, 1968, while Darryl Sittler of the Toronto Maple Leafs duplicated the feat on February 7th, 1976.

14 Roy Worters of the New York Americans captured NHL MVP honors in 1929, becoming the first goalie to win the award.

15 On March 21st, 1973, Mahovlich scored his 500th NHL goal while toiling for the Montreal Canadiens. Mahovlich would finish his NHL career with 533 goals in total.

16 Larry Robinson appeared in the Stanley Cup Playoffs from 1973 until 1992, 20 years in succession.

QUIZ 38 ANSWERS

1 Brian "Spinner" Spencer played in over 500 NHL games in his career. Spencer's life ended tragically when he was murdered on June 3rd, 1988.

2 Orr played six games for the Chicago Blackhawks during the 1978-79 season, before his wonky knees forced him to retire from the game he dominated.

3 Roger Crozier of the Detroit Red Wings appeared in all 70 of the Red Wings games during the 1964-65 season.

4 Mike Bossy of the New York Islanders scored the winning goal in all four of the Islanders' victories in the 1983 Conference Final versus the Boston Bruins.

5 Defenseman Borje Salming was named to the NHL's 1976-77 First All-Star Team.

6 The Philadelphia Flyers chose Forsberg with the sixth overall pick of the 1991 NHL Entry Draft.

7 Jean Beliveau of the Montreal Canadiens was runner-up for the Hart Trophy in 1957, 1966, 1968 and 1969. Beliveau won the Hart in both 1956 and 1964.

8 John Madden of the Devils captured the Selke Trophy in 2001 out-polling runner-up Joe Sakic of the Colorado Avalanche.

9 The 1970-71 Boston Bruins saw Phil Esposito with 152 points, Bobby Orr with 139, John Bucyk with 116 and Ken Hodge with 105, become the first NHL team to boast four 100 point men in the same regular season.

10 The Ottawa Senators defeated the Boston Bruins in four games to claim the 1927 Stanley Cup title.

11 Paul Coffey of the Edmonton Oilers scored 9 times while his team was a man short during the 1985-86 season.

12 Campbell took over from Mervyn "Red" Dutton as President of the NHL to begin the 1946-47 season. Dutton was President of the league from 1942-43 until 1945-46.

13 The Sabres called the Memorial Auditorium home for more the 25 years.

14 Vladislav Tretiak of the Soviet Union took home MVP honors in the 1981 Canada Cup.

15 All born in Kitchener, Ontario, Woody Dumart, Milt Schmidt and Bobby Bauer played on a line together beginning in junior hockey with the St. Michaels Majors. They continued to play as a unit for the NHL's Bruins, becoming one of the most famous forward lines of all time.

16 Al Arbour wore thick glasses during his playing days in the NHL. Arbour would play 626 games in his NHL career and was a member of three Stanley Cup Champions as a player.

QUIZ 39 ANSWERS

1 The Devils have won the Stanley Cup three times. New Jersey captured Lord Stanley's jug in 1995, 2000 and 2003.

2 The Flyers chose Mel Bridgman from the Western Hockey League's Victoria Cougars with the first selection of the 1975 NHL Entry Draft.

3 Wayne Gretzky scored 122 goals in his playoff career while Mark Messier with 109, Jari Kurri with 106 and Brett Hull with 103 all scored more than 100 times during their Stanley Cup Playoff careers.

4 In 1992-93, Jimmy Carson played 52 games for the Detroit Red Wings before being traded to the Los Angeles Kings where he played the final 34 games of the 1992-93 schedule. Bob Kudelski began the 1993-94 season playing 42 games for the Ottawa Senators and following a trade to Florida, played a further 44 games as a member of the Panthers.

5 Marcel Dionne of the Detroit Red Wings scored 10 of his 47 goals in the 1974-75 season, while his Wings were a man short.

6 On February 17th, 2000, McSorley viciously connected with the head of Donald Brashear of the Vancouver Canucks, with his stick, leaving Brashear convulsing on the ice.

7 Andre Lacroix scored 251 goals and added 547 assists for 798 points in just 551 games to become the leading scorer in WHA history.

8 Stan Mikita recorded all 1467 of his NHL points as a member of the Blackhawks, while Bobby Hull with 1153 points and Denis Savard with 1096 points also achieved the milestone.

9 Jacques Demers was the Montreal coach in 1993 when the Canadiens defeated the Los Angeles Kings in the Stanley Cup Final.

10 Tony Esposito recorded 76 shutouts in his stellar NHL career, hence the nickname.

11 The Toronto Maple Leafs trailed the Detroit Red Wings three games to none in the 1942 Stanley Cup Final. The Leafs reeled off four consecutive victories to complete the magnificent comeback.

12 Dave Schultz of the Philadelphia Flyers received 472 minutes in penalties in 1974-75 and 405 minutes in 1977-78. Paul Baxter of the Pittsburgh Penguins was penalized 409 minutes in 1981-82 and Mike Peluso of the Chicago Blackhawks spent 408 minutes in the sin bin in 1991-92.

13 Hector "Toe" Blake of the Montreal Canadiens would score 235 goals and was named to the NHL's First All-Star Team three times during his playing career.

14 Mario Lemieux of the Pittsburgh Penguins won the Hart Trophy in 1988, ending Gretzky's record run.

15 Canada has won the Olympic Gold in hockey six times. The Canadians were victorious in 1924, 1928, 1932, 1948, 1952 and 2002.

16 The Flyers' Reggie Leach scored 61 times to lead the NHL in 1975-76.

QUIZ 40 ANSWERS

1 The Quebec Nordiques chose Owen Nolan from the Cornwall Royals of the Ontario Hockey League with the first pick of the 1990 Entry Draft.

2 Dickie Moore of the Montreal Canadiens scored 41 goals and added 55 assists for 96 points in 1958-59 to establish the NHL record. Moore's point total would stand as a record until 1965-66 when the Chicago Blackhawks' Bobby Hull would eclipse the mark with 97 points.

3 The Calgary Flames in 1989, Dallas Stars in 1999 and the Tampa Lightning in 2004 have all won the Stanley Cup just the once.

4 Pelle Lindbergh was perhaps the finest Swedish-born goaltender to play in the National Hockey League. Lindbergh captured the Vezina Trophy in 1985 and was thought to have solved the Flyers goaltending woes for years to come.

5 Brian Leetch of the New York Rangers was named the MVP of the 1994 Stanley Cup Playoffs.

6 Kevin Stevens of the Pittsburgh Penguins scored 123 points and accumulated 254 minutes in penalties during the 1991-92 schedule.

7 Smyth played for the Moose Jaw Warriors of the WHL from 1992 until 1995.

8 The Blues acquired Brendan Shanahan in a straight up deal with the Whalers for Pronger.

9 Jean Beliveau scored 79 goals and added 97 assists for 176 points in his 162 Stanley Cup Playoff games as a member of the Habitants.

10 Gordie Howe scored 801 goals in his 26 NHL seasons and Wayne Gretzky scored 894 times in his 20 years in the league.

11 Lester Patrick coached the Rangers from 1926-27 until 1938-39.

12 Alex Delvecchio by the Detroit Red Wings, Guy Lafleur by the Montreal Canadiens and Ron Francis by the Carolina Hurricanes are the only players to have their number 10 jersey retired by an NHL team.

13 John LeClair of the Philadelphia Flyers scored 51 goals in 1995-96, 50 in 1996-97 and 51 in 1997-98.

14 Jaromir Jagr scored the 500th goal of his NHL career on February 4th, 2003, in a 5-1 Washington victory over the Tampa Bay Lightning.

15 Dick Irvin coached the Maple Leafs to Stanley Cup victory in 1932 and was coach of the Montreal Canadiens for their Stanley Cup wins in 1944, 1946 and 1953.

16 Lorne "Gump" Worsley played without the protection of a mask throughout his National Hockey career.

QUIZ 41 ANSWERS

1 Paul Reinhart of the Calgary Flames scored three times in a Stanley Cup game on April 14th, 1983 and repeated the feat on April 8th, 1984.

2 Bill Barber holds the Flyers' career goal scoring record. Barber scored 420 times in his 903 games as a member of the Flyers.

3 Alex Delvecchio, who played all 1549 games of his NHL career with the Detroit Red Wings, helping the Wings to three Stanley Cup titles in the 1950s.

4 Doug Harvey won the Norris Trophy six times while a member of the Montreal Canadiens and once as a New York Ranger. Chris Chelios captured the Norris once as a Canadien and twice as a Chicago Blackhawk. Paul Coffey won the award twice with the Edmonton Oilers and once with the Detroit Red Wings.

5 Syl Apps was named the National Hockey League's rookie of the year in 1937. Apps' Toronto teammate Gordie Drillon finished second in the Calder Trophy voting in 1937.

6 The 1951 Stanley Cup Final between the Toronto Maple Leafs and the Montreal Canadiens saw each of the five games in the series go into overtime. The Maple Leafs prevailed in the Final winning the series four games to one.

7 Wren Blair was behind the bench for the North Stars in 1967-68.

8 Jaromir Jagr of the Pittsburgh Penguins won the Pearson Award in 1999 and 2000.

9 Billy Smith won the Vezina Trophy in 1982.

10 Jim Schoenfeld, who led the Devils to the Stanley Cup Conference Finals in 1988, where they were defeated by the Boston Bruins in seven hard fought and emotional games.

11 Dany Heatley of the Atlanta Thrashers took home NHL rookie of the year honors in 2002.

12 George Armstrong was named captain of the Maple Leafs to begin the 1957-58 season and would remain the team's captain until his retirement at the conclusion of the 1968-69 schedule.

13 Al MacInnis won the James Norris Trophy in 1999 and Chris Pronger would capture the Trophy the following year.

14 Despite the fact that he was hindered by bad knees, Bobby Orr was brilliant in leading the Canadians to victory in the 1976 Canada Cup.

15 Wayne Gretzky with 382 , Mark Messier with 295, Jari Kurri with 233 and Glenn Anderson with 214 are the only players to record over 200 points in their Stanley Cup Playoff careers.

16 Gary Smith of the California Golden Seals lost 48 games in 1970-71 to set the record.

QUIZ 42 ANSWERS

1 From 1964-65 until 1978-79, the Montreal Canadiens reached and won the Stanley Cup Final ten times. Yvan Cournoyer was the only Canadien to participate in all ten Cup victories.

2 Patrick Roy was unquestionably one of the finest playoff goaltenders in the history of the National Hockey League.

3 In 1988-89, Roenick played his only season in QMJHL as a member of the Hull Olympiques where he recorded 70 points in just 28 games.

4 Mark Messier captained the Edmonton Oilers to the Stanley Cup in 1990 and wore the "C" for the New York Rangers when they won the Stanley Cup Championship in 1994.

5 The Senators sent power forward Marian Hossa and defenseman Greg deVries to the Thrashers for Heatley.

6 Phil Esposito by Boston, Ted Lindsay by Detroit, Rod Gilbert by New York and Howie Morenz by Montreal have all been honored by their respective teams by having their number 7s retired.

7 Charlie Simmer of the Los Angeles Kings scored 17 goals during his incredible 13-game goal scoring streak.

8 Steve Yzerman of the Detroit Red Wings has been a fixture in "Motown" his entire NHL career.

9   Hockey Hall of Famer Harry Lumley suited up for every Original Six club except the Montreal Canadiens, during his lengthy NHL career.

10   The six Sutter brothers combined for 1319 NHL goals. Brent led the way with 363 followed by Brian with 303, Ron 204, Darryl 161, Rich 149 and Duane with 139.

11   The United States has captured the Olympic Gold Medal twice, first in 1960 in Squaw Valley, California and once more on home soil when they finished atop the world at the 1980 Winter Olympic Games in Lake Placid, New York.

12   Rene Robert scored 40 goals and added 60 assists for 100 points during the 1974-75 season.

13   Brad Richards of the Tampa Bay Lightning won both the Lady Byng and Conn Smythe Trophies in 2004.

14   On November 12th, 1931, the Maple Leafs took on the Chicago Blackhawks in the first NHL game played at the Gardens. The Blackhawks would also be the Leafs' opponent in the final NHL game there on February 13th, 1999.

15   Scott Stevens played 1635 games in the NHL followed by Larry Murphy with 1615 and Raymond Bourque with 1612.

16   Detroit has been known as "Hockeytown" since the mid 1990s.

QUIZ 43 ANSWERS

1 Sergei Fedorov of the Detroit Red Wings scored all five of the Wings' goals in a 5-4 victory over the Washington Capitals on December 26th, 1996.

2 Pete Peeters of the Philadelphia Flyers went 27 games without suffering a loss during the 1979-80 NHL schedule and was undefeated in 31 straight starts for the Boston Bruins in 1982-83.

3 Howie Morenz of the Montreal Canadiens, like Babe Ruth in baseball, was hockey's first real superstar. Morenz's wizardry brought fans throughout the NHL to their feet.

4 Gilbert Perreault scored all 512 of his NHL career goals for the Sabres.

5 Rick Nash was a member of the OHL's London Knights from 2000 until 2002.

6 Martin Brodeur of the New Jersey Devils recorded seven shutouts during the 2003 Stanley Cup Playoffs.

7 The Minnesota Fighting Saints were members of the WHA from 1972 until 1977.

8 The volatile Darcy Tucker of the Toronto Maple Leafs has at times let his emotions get the better of him.

9 Tim Horton of the Buffalo Sabres was returning to Buffalo following a game in Toronto when his sports car went out of control on the Queen Elizabeth Way.

10 118 of Phil Esposito's 717 career NHL goals proved to be game winners.

11 Red Kelly won the Lady Byng Trophy as a defenseman with the Detroit Red Wings in 1951, 1953 and 1954. Kelly would also capture the award as a Toronto Maple Leaf forward in 1961.

12 Al Rollins of the last place Chicago Blackhawks won the 1953-54 Hart Trophy. Rollins was spectacular in goal for the Hawks despite the fact that the club lost a dismal 51 times that season.

13 The Canadiens' Maurice "Rocket" Richard scored 5 goals and added 3 assists on December 28th, 1944 and Bert Olmstead had 4 goals and 4 assists in a game on January 9th, 1954.

14 The St. Louis Blues' Garry Unger in 1974, Mike Liut in 1981 and Brett Hull in 1992 were all chosen MVP of the NHL All-Star game.

15 The Wild announced the signing of Jacques Lemaire as the club's first head coach in June of 2000. Lemaire remains to this day the only coach in Wild history.

16 In 1982, Dale Hawerchuk became the first member of the Jets to win the Calder Trophy and Teemu Selanne would capture the Trophy in 1993.

QUIZ 44 ANSWERS

1 Denis Potvin of the New York Islanders recorded his 915th point of his NHL career on December 20th, 1985, breaking Orr's record of 914.

2 Wayne Gretzky scored 73 times in his fabulous career while his team was at least a man down.

3 The 1968-69 Chicago Blackhawks saw Bobby Hull score a league record 58 times and got 30 goals apiece from Stan Mikita, Eric Nesterenko, Dennis Hull and Kenny Wharram.

4 Patrick Roy took home the Conn Smythe Trophy in both 1986 and 1993 as a member of the Montreal Canadiens and would cap his outstanding career by capturing the 2001 Conn Smythe as a member of the Colorado Avalanche.

5 Milt Schmidt spent 37 years in the Boston organization, as a player, coach and general manager.

6 Rick DiPietro was chosen by the New York Islanders with the first selection of the 2000 Entry Draft and Marc-Andre Fleury went first overall to the Pittsburgh Penguins in 2003.

7 Joe Malone of the Quebec Bulldogs scored 7 times in a game on January 31st, 1920 in a 10-6 victory over Toronto.

8 Ken Dryden won NHL rookie of the year honors in 1972.

9 Bill "Red" Hay, Bobby Hull and Murray Balfour led the Hawks to the 1961 Stanley Cup Championship.

10 Jeff Beukeboom of the New York Rangers suffered a concussion as the result of Johnson's sucker shot.

11 The Ottawa Senators set the NHL record between October 10th, 1992 and April 3rd 1993, a total of 38 road games without a single point.

12 Bobby Hull finished runner-up to Toronto Maple Leaf forward Frank Mahovlich in 1957-58.

13 Bobby Orr of the Boston Bruins was an NHL record Plus 124 during the 1970-71 season and Larry Robinson of the Montreal Canadiens recorded a Plus 120 in 1976-77.

14 Phil Esposito of the Boston Bruins recorded 152 points in 1970-71, Steve Yzerman of the Detroit Red Wings had 155 points in 1988-89 and Bernie Nicholls of the Los Angeles Kings totaled 150 points in the 1988-89 season.

15 Pat Quinn was voted the NHL's coach of the year in 1979-80 while behind the bench for the Philadelphia Flyers and again in 1991-92 while with the Vancouver Canucks.

16 The New York Islanders won 19 consecutive playoff series beginning in the first round of the 1980 Stanley Cup Playoffs, before losing to the Edmonton Oilers in the 1984 Stanley Cup Final, four games to one.

QUIZ 45 ANSWERS

1 On February 5th, 1994, Peter Bondra of the Washington Capitals scored four times in a span of just four minutes and twelve seconds, in a 6-3 victory over the Tampa Bay Lightning.

2 Frank Mahovlich was known as "The Big M" while his not so small brother Peter was known as "The Little M".

3 Philadelphia chose Ron Sutter with the 4th overall selection of the 1982 NHL Entry Draft and Pittsburgh selected his twin brother Rich with the 10th overall pick of the 1982 Draft.

4 In 1964-1965, Johnny Bower and Terry Sawchuk of the Toronto Maple Leafs allowed a combined total of 173 goals to claim the Vezina Trophy.

5 Mike Bossy of the New York Islanders scored the Stanley Cup-winning goal in both 1982 and 1983.

6 Mario Lemieux of the Pittsburgh Penguins scored 31 power play goals in both 1988-89 and 1995-96.

7 Rick Middleton of the Bruins was penalized a total of 12 minutes during the 1981-82 season. Middleton's 51 goals and 43 assists along with minimal penalty total led to his being voted winner of the 1982 Lady Byng Trophy.

8 Ken Linseman was a persistent thorn in the side of opponents throughout his 14 year NHL career.

9 Gordie Howe leads all NHLers with 1767 games played followed by Mark Messier at 1756 and Ron Francis at 1731.

10 The Montreal Canadiens' brilliant Guy Lafleur, literally "the flower" in English, was the dominant NHL player throughout the 1970s.

11 The Minnesota Wild were down 3 games to 1 in both the first and second rounds of the 2003 Stanley Cup Playoffs. The Wild came back to defeat the Colorado Avalanche in round one and the Vancouver Canucks in round two.

12 Willie O'Ree played two games for the Boston Bruins in the 1957-58 season and 43 more for the Bruins in 1960-61.

13 The Toronto Toros were members of the World Hockey Association from 1973 until 1976.

14 Alexander Yakushev led the Russians in scoring accumulating 11 points in the 8 game series.

15 Paul Coffey of the Edmonton Oilers recorded at least one point in 28 straight games during the 1985-86 season. Coffey had 16 goals and 39 assists during his incredible run.

16 Dale Hunter was penalized 729 minutes in his 186 career playoff games.

QUIZ 46 ANSWERS

1 In 1950-51, Terry Sawchuk of the Detroit Red Wings won 44 games in the 70 game schedule, to establish the rookie record.

2 Denis Potvin won rookie of the year honors in the National Hockey League in 1974.

3 On January 10th, 1920, Newsy Lalonde became the first and only member of the Habitants to score six times in game.

4 Pavel Bure scored 60 goals for the Canucks during the 1992-93 regular season.

5 On January 20th, 1983, Sittler recorded his 1000th NHL point while playing for the Philadelphia Flyers. Sittler would finish his career with 1121 points in total.

6 Steve Yzerman in 1989 and Sergei Fedorov in 1994, are the only Red Wings to win the Pearson Award.

7 On April 12th, 1986, Mike Bossy of the New York Islanders scored his 83rd Stanley Cup Playoff goal eclipsing Richard's record set 26 years earlier.

8 Scott Stevens began his NHL career with Washington Capitals and played 601 games for the team. Stevens would conclude his career as a member of the New Jersey Devils having played 956 games for the club. Al MacInnis played 803 games with the Calgary Flames and 613 as a member of the St. Louis Blues.

9 The Red Wings got Dominik Hasek in the Kozlov deal with the Sabres. Hasek would backstop Detroit to the Stanley Cup Championship in 2002.

10 On December 31st, 1988, Mario Lemieux of the Pittsburgh Penguins scored the five different ways in an 8-6 victory over the New Jersey Devils.

11 Wayne Gretzky won the Hart Trophy eight times while a member of the Edmonton Oilers and once as a Los Angeles King and Gordie Howe of the Detroit Red Wings captured the Hart six times in his remarkable career.

12 The Mighty Ducks selected Paul Kariya from the University of Maine with the 4th overall choice in the 1993 NHL Entry Draft.

13 The Rangers previously retired the number 1 of Ed Giacomin, number 7 of Rod Gilbert and the number 35 of goaltender Mike Richter.

14 Randy McKay and John Madden each fired four goals as the Devils swamped the Pittsburgh Penguins 9-0.

15 Canada defeated Russia in the gold medal game in both 2005 and 2006 to claim World Junior Hockey supremacy.

16 Marty McSorley spent a total of 3381 minutes in the penalty box in his 17 year NHL career.

QUIZ 47 ANSWERS

1 Brad Richards of the Tampa Bay Lightning scored seven game winning goals in the 2004 Stanley Cup Playoffs, leading the Lightning to their first Stanley Cup title.

2 Shutt's Montreal teammate Guy Lafleur was renowned for his pre-game rituals.

3 Nikolai Khabibulin , who led the Tampa Bay Lightning to Stanley Cup victory in 2004, before signing with the Chicago Blackhawks as a free agent in 2005.

4 Lindy Ruff took over as the Sabres head coach to begin the 1997-98 season and remains the Sabres head man to this day.

5 Jean-Sebastien Giguere of the Mighty Ducks of Anaheim shut out the Minnesota Wild in three straight games leading the Ducks to a four game sweep of the Wild in the 2003 Stanley Cup Semi-Finals.

6 Chicago-born Chris Chelios was selected to the NHL First All-Star Team once as a member of the Montreal Canadiens, three times as a Chicago Blackhawk and once with the Detroit Red Wings.

7 Phaneuf played for the Red Deer Rebels of the WHL. Phaneuf was chosen 9th overall in 2003 NHL Entry Draft by the Calgary Flames.

8 The Boston Bruins' Bobby Orr in 1967 and Derek Sanderson in 1968 were the last teammates to win rookie of the year honors in consecutive seasons.

9 Henri Richard of the Montreal Canadiens was a member of eleven Stanley Cup winners and brother Maurice was with the Habitants for eight of their Stanley Cup titles.

10 Although he never played a game in the National Hockey League, Vladislav Tretiak became the first Russian member of the Hall of Fame with his induction in 1989.

11 The Canadiens acquired Lou Fontinato from the Rangers for Harvey. Harvey would go on to win the Norris Trophy as the NHL's best defenseman in 1961-62 while Fontinato would lead the NHL in penalty minutes that season.

12 Goaltender Pelle Lindbergh of the Philadelphia Flyers and right winger Jari Kurri were named to the NHL's 1984-85 First All-Star Team.

13 With remarks such as "Old Blinky was flying tonight", Gordie Howe made light of a severe brain injury he received in an NHL game in 1950, that left him with a slight facial tic.

14 Doug Gilmour scored 27 goals and added 84 assists for 111 points during the 1993-94 NHL schedule.

15 In the 1992-93 season, Kevin Hatcher scored 34 goals, Al Iafrate tallied 25 and Sylvain Cote scored 21 times for the Washington Capitals.

16 Swedish forward Kent Nilsson of the Calgary Flames scored 49 goals and added 82 assists for 131 points during the 1980-81 NHL schedule.

QUIZ 48 ANSWERS

1 The 1987 NHL Entry Draft was held at the Joe Louis Arena in Detroit, Michigan.

2 At 6' 3", 214 pounds, Elmer "Moose" Vasko used his size and strength to carve out a productive 13-year NHL career.

3 The Ottawa Nationals were members of the WHA for only the 1972-73 season.

4 In 1949, Bill Quackenbush of the Detroit Red Wings became the first rearguard to win the Lady Byng Trophy. Red Kelly of the Red Wings would capture the award as a defenseman in 1951, 1952 and 1954.

5 Goalkeeper Patrick Roy was the last Montreal Canadien to be selected to the NHL's First All-Star Team when he was named to the 1991-92 squad.

6 In 2002, for the first time in NHL history, two players tied in voting for the Hart Trophy. Jose Theodore of the Montreal Canadiens and Jerome Iginla of the Calgary Flames each received 434 votes in the Hart balloting. Theodore was awarded the trophy based on more first place votes (26 to 23).

7 On March 11th, 2003, Housley was traded by the Chicago Blackhawks to the Toronto Maple Leafs. Housley played in just one regular season game for the Leafs and called it a career following three playoff games with the Leafs.

8 Harry Lumley was often referred to as 'Apple Cheeks'.

9 Billy Smith of the New York Islanders was the last Islander to touch the puck when Rob Ramage of the Colorado Rockies shot the disc into his own net in a game on November 28th, 1979.

10 Both Jean Beliveau and Henri Richard played twenty seasons with the Canadiens.

11 Team Canada's Darryl Sittler beat Czechoslovakian goaltender Vladamir Dzurilla at 11:03 of overtime to give Canada a 5-4 win in the game and a 2-0 victory in the final series.

12 Bobby Orr played with tremendous poise and vision in the game he dominated for the better part of a decade.

13 Bobby Clarke in 1973 was the first Flyer to win the Pearson Award and Eric Lindros became the only other Flyer to win the award when he was judged the NHL's outstanding player by his peers in 1995.

14 Ray Sheppard scored at least 20 goals in a season with the Buffalo Sabres, New York Rangers, Detroit Red Wings, San Jose Sharks, Florida Panthers and Carolina Hurricanes. Sheppard would score a total of 357 goals in his 13 NHL seasons.

15 The Maple Leafs sent Frank Mahovlich, Garry Unger, Pete Stemkowski and the rights to Carl Brewer to the Red Wings.

16 Mike Peca won the Selke Trophy in 1997 as a member of the Buffalo Sabres, and again captured the award in 2002 while playing for the New York Islanders.

QUIZ 49 ANSWERS

1 Hector "Toe" Blake was the head coach of the Canadiens for their five consecutive Stanley Cup titles from 1956 until 1960.

2 The Canucks retired Stan Smyl's number 12. Smyl played his entire NHL career with Vancouver and retired as the Canucks' all time leader in games played with 896 and points scored with 673.

3 Bryan Berard was selected first overall in the 1995 NHL Entry Draft by the Ottawa Senators and would go on to win NHL rookie of the year honors in 1997 as a member of the New York Islanders.

4 Dave Andreychuk scored 274 times in his NHL career while his team enjoyed a man advantage.

5 Derek Sanderson of the Boston Bruins was considered to be the NHL's premier playboy during the 1960s and early 1970s.

6 Pavel Bure of the Vancouver Canucks scored three penalty shot goals during the 1997-98 NHL regular season.

7 Scotty Bowman coached the St. Louis Blues to the Stanley Cup Finals in 1968, 1969 and 1970. The Blues lost both the 1968 and 1969 Cup Finals to the Montreal Canadiens 4-0 and were again swept by the Boston Bruins in the 1970 Cup Final.

8 The 1929-30 Boston Bruins won 20 games in succession and would go on to lose only once at home during the season.

9 Gordie Howe played for the Detroit Red Wings from 1946-47 until 1970-71 a total of 25 seasons and Alex Delvecchio played 24 seasons for the Red Wings from 1950-51 until 1973-74.

10 George Armstrong played 1187 games with the Maple Leafs followed by Tim Horton at 1185, Borje Salming at 1099, Dave Keon at 1062 and Ron Ellis at 1034.

11 Wayne Gretzky of the Edmonton Oilers scored 92 times during the 1981-82 schedule to set the record that many experts feel is unbreakable.

12 Maurice Richard of the Montreal Canadiens scored 544 goals added 421 assists for 965 points.

13 Roger Neilson was considered to be a major innovator in coaching during his 1000 games behind an NHL bench.

14 Vincent Damphousse of the Maple Leafs took home MVP honors in the 1991 NHL All-Star game.

15 The Jets won the Avco Cup three times in the WHA's brief history. The Jets first won the League Championship in 1976 and would win back to back titles in 1978 and 1979.

16 Doug Harvey, Pierre Pilote, Bobby Orr and Nicklas Lidstrom all captured the Norris Trophy at least three years in a row.

QUIZ 50 ANSWERS

1 Ulf Samuelsson was known throughout the NHL as a notorious cheap-shot artist. Samuelsson's knee-on-knee hit on Boston's Cam Neely virtually ended Neely's fine career.

2 The Senators selected Alexei Yashin from Moscow Dynamo with their first pick of the 1992 Entry Draft.

3 Paul Coffey established the Oilers franchise record of 138 points during the 1985-86 season and set the Penguins mark with 113 points in 1988-89.

4 Raymond Bourque appeared in 19 NHL All-Star games. Bourque made his first appearance in 1981 and would play in his last All-Star game in 2001.

5 Phil Esposito of the Boston Bruins won the first Pearson Award in 1971.

6 Scotty Bowman held the position of coach/general manager of the Detroit Red Wings when they captured the Stanley Cup in 1997.

7 From 1974 until 1980 inclusive, the Soviet Union won the gold medal at the World Junior Hockey Championships.

8 Teemu Selanne of the Winnipeg Jets scored 76 goals and added 56 assists for 132 points during the 1992-93 season and Alexander Ovechkin of the Washington Capitals scored 52 times and added 54 assists for 106 points during the 2005-06 NHL campaign.

9 Brett Hull scored 527 goals in just 744 games as a member of the Blues.

10 Eddie Shack of the Toronto Maple Leafs was voted MVP of the 1962 All-Star game. Shack's Maple Leafs defeated the NHL All-Stars 4-1 in the game played at Maple Leaf Gardens.

11 The Panthers selected Ed Jovanovski from the Windsor Spitfires of the Ontario Hockey League with the first choice of the 1994 NHL Entry Draft.

12 Chicoutimi, Quebec born, Georges Vezina was forced to retire in 1925 because of tuberculosis after appearing in 325 consecutive regular season games with the Montreal

13 Brian Leetch of the New York Rangers scored 23 times in 1988-89, to establish the rookie record.

14 Trudeau felt that Jean Beliveau of the Montreal Canadiens possessed all the qualities that constitute greatness.

15 Hull played the final nine games of his NHL career with the Hartford Whalers during the 1979-80 season.

16 Although Allan Stanley, Tim Horton, Carl Brewer and Borje Salming have all been runner-up in voting for the Norris Trophy, the Maple Leafs have yet to have a member of the club win the coveted Trophy.

QUIZ 51 ANSWERS

1 Dit Clapper played 20 seasons with the Boston Bruins. Clapper began his NHL career in 1927-28 and ended his tenure in the league in 1946-47.

2 Phil Esposito recorded his 1500th NHL point in 1979-80, while a member of the New York Rangers. Esposito would finish his NHL career in 1980-81 with a total 1590 points.

3 The Boston Bruins won 57 games in 1970-71, 54 games in 1971-72, 51 games in 1972-73 and 52 games in 1973-74.

4 Lou Nanne played eleven season in the National Hockey League in the 1960s and 1970s, all with the Minnesota North Stars.

5 Wayne Gretzky captured the Lady Byng Trophy five times during his magnificent career. Gretzky won the 1980 Byng Trophy with the Edmonton Oilers, won it in 1991, 1992 and 1994 as a member of the Los Angeles Kings and won it for the last time in 1999 as a New York Ranger.

6 Bernie Geoffrion was the first coach of the Atlanta Flames. Geoffrion coached the team from 1972 until midway through the 1974-75 schedule.

7 Brett Hull scored 38 times in his 202 career playoff games, while his team enjoyed a man advantage.

8 The Maple Leafs received Leonard "Red" Kelly from the Red Wings. Kelly would help Toronto to four Stanley Cup Championships in the 1960s while Reaume would contribute very little in his short stay (47 games) with the Red Wings.

9 Ron Francis, Sylvain Turgeon and Kevin Dineen formed the Whalers "FTD" line.

10 Brit Selby won the Calder Trophy in 1966. Selby would go on to have a rather undistinguished NHL career considering the future expectations placed on Calder Trophy winners.

11 Dino Ciccarelli scored 73 goals in just 141 Stanley Cup Playoff games, however Ciccarelli finished his NHL career having never won hockey's ultimate prize.

12 The Blackhawks have won the Stanley Cup three times in franchise history. The Hawks won the Stanley Cup in 1934, 1938 and 1961.

13 Bobby Orr of the Boston Bruins became the first NHL defenseman to score at least 40 times in a season when he scored 46 times in 1974-75. Paul Coffey of the Edmonton Oilers would score 40 times in 1983-84 and light the lamp an NHL record 48 times in 1985-86.

14 Syl Apps has been inducted into the Hockey Hall of Fame, the Canadian Sports Hall of Fame and Canadian Amateur Athletics Hall of fame.

15 Maurice "Rocket" Richard led the NHL in goal scoring in 1944-45, 1946-47, 1949-50, 1953-54 and 1954-55.

16 Peter Stastny of the Quebec Nordiques scored 39 goals and added 70 assists for 109 points in the 1980-81 NHL regular season.

QUIZ 52 ANSWERS

1 From March 9th until April 10th, 1993, the Pittsburgh Penguins won 17 consecutive games breaking the New York Islanders record of 15 straight wins established in 1982.

2 Glenn Hall by the Chicago Blackhawks, Terry Sawchuk by the Detroit Red Wings, Jacques Plante by the Montreal Canadiens, Ed Giacomin by the New York Rangers and Bernie Parent by the Philadelphia Flyers have all seen their number 1 retired.

3 Bruce Gamble of the Toronto Maple Leafs took home MVP honors in the 1968 NHL All-Star game.

4 Markus Naslund of the Canucks was voted as the NHL's MVP by the NHLPA in 2003.

5 Although he often appeared to be slow afoot, Doug Harvey of the Montreal Canadiens used his uncanny ability and patience with the puck to dominate the game like no other NHL defenseman before him.

6 Bobby Baun of the Maple Leafs returned from the infirmary to score the overtime winner. Baun, it would later be learned, scored his goal while playing on a broken leg. The Maple Leafs rode Baun's heroics to a 4-0 victory in Game 7 thus capturing the Stanley Cup.

7 The Vancouver Canucks selected Swedish twin brothers Daniel and Henrik Sedin with the second and third overall pick of the 1999 NHL Entry Draft.

8 Patrick Roy played in a total of 247 Stanley Cup Playoff games with the Montreal Canadiens and the Colorado Avalanche.

9 Bossy played for the Laval National of the QMJHL from 1973 until 1977 accumulating an astounding 309 goals during his junior career.

10 Bruce Hood officiated in his 1000th NHL game on November 19th, 1983.

11 The 1937-38 Chicago Blackhawks squeaked into the Stanley Cup Playoffs with an unimpressive 14-25-9 record during the regular season. The Hawks would go on to defeat the Toronto Maple Leafs three games to one in the 1938 Stanley Cup Final.

12 Coffey played the final 18 games of his NHL career as a member of the Boston Bruins in 2000-2001.

13 Grant Fuhr won the Vezina Trophy in 1988, leading the NHL in victories with 40 and games played with 75.

14 Wayne Gretzky accomplished the feat three times (1980-81, 1983-84 and 1984-85), Mario Lemieux also did it on three occasions (1988-89, 1992-93 and 1995-96) and Brett Hull did it twice (1990-91 and 1991-92).

15 On January 16th, 1934, Ken Dorarty of the Toronto Maple Leafs scored three goals in the overtime period to give his Leafs a 7-4 victory over the Ottawa Senators. Overtime was a 10 minute mandatory period in 1934, not sudden death.

16 Frank Boucher of the New York Rangers won the Lady Byng Trophy from 1928 to 1931 and from 1933 to 1935. The NHL was forced to craft a new Lady Byng Trophy to honor the 1936 recipient of the award.

QUIZ 53 ANSWERS

1 Marcel Dionne may have been small in stature but his incredible skill allowed him to score 731 goals during his 18-year NHL career.

2 Gordie Howe led the NHL in goal scoring in 1950-51, 1951-52, 1952-53, 1956-57 and 1962-63.

3 Tony Esposito won 418 of his 423 NHL career victories while a member of the Chicago Blackhawks

4 Duane Sutter was a member of the Stanley Cup Champion, New York Islanders from 1979-80 until 1982-83 and brother Brent was with the Islanders for Stanley Cup titles in 1981-82 and 1982-83.

5 Wayne Gretzky scored five times in a game on four occasions, while Jari Kurri and Pat Hughes both accomplished the rare feat once.

6 Tom Barrasso recorded 48 assists in his 777 NHL games in a career than spanned 19 seasons.

7 The Flyers' Bobby Clarke was voted the NHL's MVP in both 1975 and 1976.

8 The Maple Leafs acquired forward Wendel Clark and defensemen Mathieu Schneider and D.J. Smith from the Islanders. The return of Clark to the Maple Leafs was greeted with joy among the loyal fans of the team.

9 In 1987-88, rookie Joe Nieuwendyk of the Calgary Flames scored 31 times while his club enjoyed a man advantage.

10 Paul Coffey had three 100 point or better seasons while a member of the Edmonton Oilers and recorded over 100 points in a season twice while playing for the Pittsburgh Penguins.

11 Gump Worsley of the Montreal Canadiens had the pleasure of drinking from the Stanley Cup on four occasions.

12 Dave Reese of the Boston Bruins was in net as the Maple Leafs shellacked the Bruins 11-4. Reese would never play another game in the National Hockey League.

13 Sergei Fedorov won the Selke Trophy in both 1994 and 1996, while Steve Yzerman was named the NHL's outstanding defensive forward in 2000.

14 Pierre Turgeon of the New York Islanders had just scored the Series winning goal when he was blind-sided by an incensed Hunter.

15 Roger Neilson coached eight NHL teams in his coaching career: the Toronto Maple Leafs, Buffalo Sabres, Vancouver Canucks, Los Angeles Kings, New York Rangers, Florida Panthers, Philadelphia Flyers and Ottawa Senators.

16 From 1969-70 until 1974-75, Bobby Orr of the Boston Bruins scored 100 or more points in a season.

QUIZ 54 ANSWERS

1 The Panthers chose Ed Jovanovski from the Windsor Spitfires of the Ontario Hockey League with the first overall selection of the 1994 NHL Entry Draft.

2 The Maple Leafs have retired the number 5 of Bill Barilko and the number 6 of Ace Bailey.

3 Jean Beliveau of the Montreal Canadiens ended his NHL career in 1971 with a record 176 points in the Stanley Cup Playoffs.

4 The tall and rangy Larry Robinson of the Montreal Canadiens was an NHL first team All-Star three times during his career.

5 Moscow born Viacheslav Fetisov was inducted into the Hockey Hall of Fame in 2001. Fetisov won the Stanley Cup twice while a member of the Detroit Red Wings.

6 Bure retired from the NHL as a member of the New York Rangers in 2005. Bure led the NHL in goal scoring three times during his relatively short career.

7 Gordie Howe of the Detroit Red Wings from 1951 to 1954, Phil Esposito of the Boston Bruins from 1971 to 1974, Wayne Gretzky of the Edmonton Oilers from 1981 to 1987 and Jaromir Jagr of the Pittsburgh Penguins from 1998 to 2001, all won the Art Ross Trophy at least four years in succession.

8 The NHL has expanded ten times since 1967. The first expansion took place in 1967 and the last expansion occurred in 1999.

9 Twice. Sweden won the Gold Medal in the 1994 Olympic Games in Lillehammer, Norway, and again took home the Gold in Turin, Italy in 2006.

10 Jacques Plante of the Montreal Canadiens won six Stanley Cups between 1953 and 1960 and Ken Dryden of the Canadiens won six Stanley Cup Championships between 1971 and 1979.

11 Dennis Hull probably had a harder shot than his brother Bobby, but often had no idea where it was going.

12 Tim Kerr scored 50 or more goals in a season four consecutive times, the majority of them scored from in close.

13 Mario Lemieux of the Pittsburgh Penguins was named the MVP of the Stanley Cup Playoffs in both 1991 and 1992.

14 The Montreal Canadiens totaled an NHL record 132 points during the 1976-77 season. The Habitants won 60 games and tied 12 others while losing just 8 times during the 80 game schedule.

15 The Canadiens legally purchased the QHL in 1953, making Jean Beliveau their exclusive property. Up to that point, Beliveau showed little interest in playing in the NHL and was quite content to play his hockey for the QHL's Quebec Aces.

16 Wendel Clark, Gary Leeman and Russ Courtnall formed the Maple Leafs' short-lived "Hound Line". All were members of the renowned Notre Dame Hounds of Wilcox, Saskatchewan during their high school days.

QUIZ 55 ANSWERS

1 George "Punch" Imlach was behind the Sabres bench for the 1970-71 season. The Sabres would win a respectable 24 games in their inaugural season in the NHL.

2 The Senators won the Stanley Cup in 1920, 1921, 1923 and 1927 for a total of four Championships. The Senators would transfer to St. Louis to begin the 1934-35 season and Ottawa would be left without an NHL franchise for the better part of six decades.

3 On December 8th, 1987, Ron Hextall of the Philadelphia Flyers, shot the puck the length of the ice, into an empty Boston Bruins net to become the first NHL goaltender to shoot and score a goal.

4 Larry Robinson played in his 200th Stanley Cup Playoff game as a member of the Montreal Canadiens on May 19th, 1989. Robinson would play a total of 227 playoff games during his NHL career.

5 Gary Smith played for 7 different teams during his NHL career, gaining him the nickname "Suitcase".

6 Jacques Demers was the head coach of the Nordiques in their inaugural NHL season.

7 Bobby Hull of the Chicago Blackhawks scored his 600th NHL goal, late in the 1971-72 season. Hull would leave the Blackhawks for the rival World Hockey Association in 1972.

8 The Rangers sent Brad Park, Jean Ratelle and Joe Zanussi to the Bruins in perhaps the biggest trade of the decade.

9 Joe Juneau of the Boston Bruins scored 32 goals and added 70 assists for 102 points during the 1992-93 NHL schedule. Unfortunately for Juneau, Teemu Selanne of the Winnipeg Jets had the best rookie year in the history of the league, and claimed the 1993 Calder Trophy.

10 The Hawks have retired the number 1 of Glenn Hall and the number 35 of Tony Esposito.

11 In 1996, Jim Carey became the first Capital to win the Vezina Trophy and the Capitals' Olaf Kolzig would capture the award in 2000.

12 Bob Probert was considered to be the heavyweight champion of the NHL while his teammate Joey Kocur could hold his own against the best fighters in the league.

13 Marcel Dionne of the Los Angeles Kings scored 53 goals to Gretzky's 51 to claim the only NHL scoring title of his Hall of Fame career.

14 Paul Baxter was assessed 962 minutes in penalties in his 290 games in the WHA.

15 Bobby Orr in 1972, Raymond Bourque in 1996 and Bill Guerin in 2001 all were selected as the MVP of the NHL All-Star game.

16 Aurel Joliet of the Montreal Canadiens stood just 5' 7" tall and weighed under 140 pounds, however his size did not stop Joliet from scoring 270 goals in his 16 NHL seasons.

QUIZ 56 ANSWERS

1 Guy Lafleur of the Montreal Canadiens scored at least 50 times in six straight NHL seasons, from 1974-75 until 1979-80.

2 Gary Green was just 26 years of age when he was named coach of the Washington Capitals, 16 games into the 1979-80 schedule.

3 Bobby Clarke's vicious slash to Kharlamov's ankle forced the Russian speedster to miss the final two games of the 1972 Summit Series.

4 The Wild selected Czechoslovakian-born Marian Gaborik with the 3rd overall pick of the 2000 NHL Entry Draft.

5 Luc Robitaille scored 45 goals added 39 assists for 84 points in capturing the 1987 Calder Trophy.

6 In 1990-91, Ed Belfour of the Chicago Blackhawks won both the Calder Trophy and the Vezina Trophy on his way to being named to the NHL's First All-Star Team that season.

7 The 1994-95 National Hockey League season did not begin until January 20th, 1995. The late start to the season forced the league to go to an abbreviated 48 game schedule.

8 In the 1980-81 season, Kent Nilsson scored 49 goals and added 82 assists for 131 points to establish the Flames franchise record.

9 Bobby Orr of the Boston Bruins won the Pearson Award in 1975. Orr also captured the Art Ross Trophy and the Norris Trophy in 1975.

10 Lindsay was known as either "Terrible Ted" or "Scarface".

11 On March 5th, 1992, Mats Sundin scored five times in the 10-4 defeat of the Hartford Whalers and Mike Ricci potted five goals in a 8-2 crushing of the San Jose Sharks on February 17th, 1994.

12 Terry Sawchuk was the last Red Wing to win the Vezina Trophy. Detroit allowed an NHL low 134 goals in the 1954-55 season, as Sawchuk captured his third Vezina Trophy in four years.

13 The San Diego Mariners were members of the World Hockey Association from 1974 until 1977.

14 Patrick Roy won 289 times while a member of the Montreal Canadiens and registered another 262 victories backstopping the Colorado Avalanche.

15 Nels Stewart retired at the conclusion of the 1939-40 season with a then record 324 regular season NHL goals.

16 The Blues acquired future superstar Brett Hull and Steve Bozek from the Flames.

QUIZ 57 ANSWERS

1 Mario Lemieux won the Calder Trophy in 1985 outdistancing runner-up Chris Chelios of the Montreal Canadiens in the voting for the award.

2 Clark played the final 20 games of his NHL career as a member of the Toronto Maple Leafs in 2000. Clark was acquired by the team on January 14th, 2000, following his release by the Chicago Blackhawks.

3 The Montreal Canadiens won 58 games in 1975-76, 60 games in 1976-77, 59 games in 1977-78 and 52 games in 1978-79.

4 Bobby Hull's blazing speed and flowing blonde hair earned him the nickname "The Golden Jet".

5 Red Kelly won four Stanley Cups as a member of the Detroit Red Wings in the 1950s and duplicated the feat with the Toronto Maple Leafs in the 1960s.

6 Jacques Plante of the Montreal Canadiens won both trophies in 1962, and Dominik Hasek of the Buffalo Sabres won both awards in 1997 and again in 1998.

7 Johnny Bucyk of the Boston Bruins was 35 years, 10 months old when he scored his 50th goal of the 1970-71 season. Bucyk would finish the year with 51 goals.

8 Hector "Toe" Blake won exactly 500 NHL games with the Montreal Canadiens in his 13 seasons behind the Habitants bench.

9 Dickie Moore was a key member of the Montreal Canadiens 1950s dynasty.

10 The Vancouver Blazers were members of the WHA for just two seasons, 1973-74 and 1974-75.

11 Jean Ratelle recorded his 100th point of the 1971-72 NHL season on February 18th, 1972. Ratelle would finish the season with 109 points in just 63 games. Vic Hadfield also eclipsed 100 points in 1971-72, reaching the total over one month later than Ratelle.

12 The Islanders chose Billy Harris from the Toronto Marlies of the OMJHL first overall in the 1972 NHL Entry Draft.

13 From 1949-50 until 1968-69, Gordie Howe of the Detroit Red Wings was among the top 5 point producers in the NHL. Howe's streak ended in 1969-70 when he finished ninth in league scoring.

14 Lorne "Gump" Worsley lost 352 of his 861 NHL games.

15 The Tampa Bay Lightning selected Roman Hamrlik with the first pick of the 1992 Entry Draft and Alexei Yashin was chosen second overall by the Ottawa Senators.

16 Stan Mikita won the Art Ross Trophy four times in a span of five years. Mikita led the NHL in scoring in 1963-64 and 1964-65 and again won consecutive league scoring titles in 1966-67 and 1968-69.

QUIZ 58 ANSWERS

1 Patrick Roy recorded 23 shutouts in Stanley Cup play and Martin Brodeur had shut out the opponent on 20 occasions entering the 2006 Stanley Cup Playoffs.

2 Ken Dryden of the Montreal Canadiens won the Conn Smythe Trophy in 1971 and the Calder Trophy in 1972. Dryden was eligible for 1972 NHL rookie of the year honors, as he had only played six regular season games with the Habitants in the 1970-71 schedule.

3 Wayne Gretzky recorded 1669 points with the Edmonton Oilers and 918 as a member of the Los Angeles Kings. Mark Messier scored 1034 points as a member of the Oilers and 560 as a New York Ranger. Ron Francis recorded 821 points with the Hartford Whalers and 613 points with the Pittsburgh Penguins.

4 Sergei Fedorov totaled 107 points on 39 goals and 68 assists for the Red Wings during the 1995-96 season.

5 Tim Horton played for the Toronto Maple Leafs, New York Rangers, Pittsburgh Penguins and Buffalo Sabres during his 24 seasons in the National Hockey League.

6 The Maple Leafs played their NHL home games at the Mutual Street Arena prior to moving to the Gardens.

7 Mike Liut of the St. Louis Blues was voted the NHL's best player by the NHLPA in 1981. Liut would also be named to the NHL's First All-Star Team that season.

8 Gordie Howe was noted for his quick wit during post-game interviews.

9 Jari Kurri scored 601 goals and added 797 assists for 1398 points during his 1251 game NHL career.

10 Sawchuk was often called "Ukey, as the Winnipeg, Manitoba native, was of Ukranian decent.

11 Maurice "Rocket" Richard, Jean Beliveau, Frank Mahovlich and Guy Lafleur all scored career goal number 500 while members of the Habitants.

12 Mario Lemieux of the Pittsburgh Penguins scored 3 goals and added 3 assists for 6 points in the 1988 NHL All-Star game.

13 Jason Allison was the Bruins' captain for the 2000-01 season.

14 The Kings sent Jimmy Carson, Martin Gelinas, three first round draft picks and cash to the Oilers. Although the Oilers would win the Stanley Cup in 1989-90, the trade basically brought to an end the Oiler dynasty.

15 Peter Forsberg won the 1995 Calder Trophy while a member of the Quebec Nordiques and won the 2003 Hart Trophy as a member of the Colorado Avalanche.

16 Eddie Shack scored at least 20 goals in a season for the Toronto Maple Leafs, Boston Bruins, Los Angeles Kings, Buffalo Sabres and Pittsburgh Penguins.

QUIZ 59 ANSWERS

1 Ted Lindsay led the NHL in goal scoring in 1947-48, assists in 1949-50 and 1956-57, points in 1949-50 and penalty minutes in 1959-60.

2 Stan Mikita of the Chicago Blackhawks assisted on 62 goals during the 1966-67 NHL campaign.

3 John Tonelli's rugged and gritty two-way play earned him the MVP of the 1984 Canada Cup.

4 Phil Housley established the Sabres record of 81 points during the 1989-90 NHL season and set the Jets/Coyotes record of 97 points in 1992-93 while a member of the Jets.

5 Bobby Hull of the Chicago Blackhawks was named the MVP of the NHL All-Star game in both 1970 and 1971.

6 Shero felt that Bobby Clarke possessed all the qualities that made a great team leader.

7 Emile "Butch" Bouchard won four Stanley Cup titles in 1940s and 1950s as a member of the Montreal Canadiens and his son Pierre was a member of five Canadiens' Stanley Cup winners in the 1970s.

8 Wayne Gretzky won the Art Ross Trophy ten times, while Mario Lemieux captured it six times and Jaromir Jagr won it on five occasions.

9 Mike Gartner scored his 500th goal on October 14th, 1991 and Mark Messier scored number 500 of his career on November 6th, 1995.

10 Mats Sundin of the Quebec Nordiques had at least one point in 30 straight games during the 1992-93 season. Sundin scored 21 goals and added 25 assists for 46 points during his streak.

11 The Maroons won the Stanley Cup twice. The Maroons defeated Victoria in the 1926 Stanley Cup Final and prevailed over the Toronto Maple Leafs in 1935 to claim their last Stanley Cup.

12 Wayne Babych scored 54 times for the Blues during the 1980-81 NHL schedule.

13 Gretzky's Edmonton Oiler teammate Jari Kurri scored 92 of his 106 playoff goals as a member of the Oilers. Gretzky scored only 81 of his playoff total while with the Edmonton club.

14 Crosby played for the Rimouski Oceanic of the QMJHL from 2003 until 2005.

15 The New England Whalers were the first winners of the Avco Cup in 1973.

16 Kevin Stevens, John Cullen and Mark Recchi were all in the option year of their contracts with the Penguins, thus the fitting nickname.

QUIZ 60 ANSWERS

1 Patrick Lalime of the Pittsburgh Penguins went undefeated in his first 16 NHL games during the 1996-97 regular season.

2 The Boston team was known as "The Big Bad Bruins". The Bruins combined immense skill with considerable toughness to strike fear into the majority of the teams in the NHL.

3 Rookie Teemu Selanne of the Winnipeg Jets scored 76 goals in 1992-93 to tie Alexander Mogilny of the Buffalo Sabres for the NHL lead in goal scoring.

4 Guy Lafleur of the Montreal Canadiens won the Pearson Award in 1976, 1977 and 1978.

5 Howie Morenz of the Montreal Canadiens won the Hart Trophy in both 1931 and 1932.

6 Ian Turnbull scored 22 goals and added 57 assists for 79 points during the 1976-77 season, establishing the Leaf record

7 Peter Stastny of the Quebec Nordiques recorded his 1000th NHL point on October 19th, 1989, in just his 682nd NHL game.

8 Rudy Pilous was coach of the Blackhawks when they defeated the Detroit Red Wings 4 games to 2 in the 1961 Stanley Cup Final.

9 Glenn Hall was selected to the NHL's First All-Star Team, once as a member of the Detroit Red Wings, five times while with the Chicago Blackhawks and once with the St. Louis Blues.

10 Norm Ullman scored 42 goals during the 1964-65 NHL schedule.

11 Mark Messier won the Conn Smythe in 1984, Wayne Gretzky was Playoff MVP in both 1985 and 1988 and goaltender Bill Ranford won the award in 1990.

12 Doug Jarvis won the Selke Trophy in 1984 outdistancing runner-up Bryan Trottier of the New York Islanders in voting for the award.

13 Gerry Cheevers won 229 NHL games as a member of the Boston Bruins, backstopping the team to two Stanley Cup titles in the 1970s.

14 Maurice "Rocket" Richard scored five times once and twice tallied four goals in a Stanley Cup Playoff game.

15 Evgeni Nabokov won the Calder Trophy in 2001 becoming just the first European-trained netminder to win the Trophy.

16 From 1955 to 1964, Andy Hebenton never missed a game. Hebenton played eight full seasons with the New York Rangers and one full season with the Boston Bruins. Incredibly, the 630 consecutive games played by Hebenton constituted his entire NHL career.

1 On March 11th, 2003, the Montreal Canadiens traded Gilmour to the Toronto Maple Leafs. Gilmour suffered a serious injury in his first game back with the Leafs and would not play in the National Hockey League again.

2 Swede Stefan Persson won four consecutive Stanley Cup rings as a member of the New York Islanders, from 1980 until 1983.

3 Jean Beliveau got his nickname from a popular French folk song.

4 Bobby Orr, Bryan Trottier and Mario Lemieux are the only players to capture all four of the prestigious NHL trophys at least once.

5 Joe Malone of the Montreal Canadiens scored 44 goals in just 20 games for a 2.2 goals per game average in the 1917-18 season.

6 The United States defeated Canada two games to one in the final of the 1996 World Cup of Hockey.

7 Bill Durnan of the Montreal Canadiens was an NHL First Team All-Star from 1943-44 until 1946-47 and Ken Dryden of the Canadiens was selected to the First Team from 1975-76 until 1978-79.

8 Wayne Gretzky of the Edmonton Oilers scored eight points in a game on November 19th, 1983 and January 4th, 1984 and Mario Lemieux of the Pittsburgh Penguins recorded eight point games on October 15th, 1988 and December 31st, 1988.

9 Bernard "Boom Boom" Geoffrion would become a leader with the Canadiens but would fall short of Irvin's prediction.

10 Mark Messier captured the Pearson Award in 1990 while a member of the Edmonton Oilers and won it again in 1992 as a member of the New York Rangers.

11 The 1948-49, Toronto Maple Leafs finished the regular season with a modest record of 22 wins, 25 losses and 13 ties. The Leafs would surprise the Detroit Red Wings in the 1949 Stanley Cup Final in four games.

12 Hal Laycoe was the coach of the Canucks from 1970-71 until 1971-72.

13 Alexander Ovechkin of the Washington Capitals was given the nickname during the 2005-06 NHL season.

14 Milan Hejduk won the Richard Trophy in 2002-03, leading the NHL with 50 goals.

15 Team USA goaltender Mike Richter was a standout throughout the tournament in capturing MVP honors.

16 The CHL is comprised of the Ontario Hockey League, the Western Hockey League and the Quebec Major Junior Hockey League.

1 Phil Housley scored 338 goals and added 894 assists for 1232 points in his 21 NHL seasons.

2 Gordie Howe was inducted in 1972 and played in the NHL until 1980; Guy Lafleur in 1988 and remained in the NHL until 1991; Mario Lemieux in 1997 and officially retired from the NHL on January 24th, 2006.

3 The Stars' Jere Lehtinen won the Selke Trophy in 1998, 1999 and 2003.

4 Marcel Dionne recorded 1771 regular season points, but played in only 49 post season games and never played on a Stanley Cup Championship team.

5 Left winger Bobby Hull of the Chicago Blackhawks from 1963-64 until 1969-70 and centerman Wayne Gretzky of the Edmonton Oilers from 1980-81 until 1986-87.

6 Henri Richard of the Montreal Canadiens played on an NHL record eleven Stanley Cup Championship teams.

7 Charlie Conacher of the Toronto Maple Leafs led the NHL in scoring in 1933-34 and 1934-34 while his brother Roy won the Art Ross Trophy in 1948-49. Doug Bentley of the Chicago Blackhawks led the league in points in 1942-1943 and brother Max of the Blackhawks was the NHL's top point producer in both 1945-46 and 1946-47.

8 Pavel Bure with 60 goals in 1993-94 for the Vancouver Canucks, and with 58 and 59 goals for the Florida Panthers in 1999-2000 and 2000-01 respectively.

9 Chris "Knuckles" Nilan, who twice led the NHL in penalty minutes in a season.

10 Bryan Trottier of the New York Islanders recorded at least one point in 18 consecutive games during the 1981 Stanley Cup Playoffs. Trottier had 11 goals and 18 assists during his record streak.

11 23. They also captured the Stanley Cup in 1916, prior to the formation of the NHL.

12 Andre Lacroix played for five different WHA teams from 1972 until 1979, appearing in 551 games.

13 Harry Howell of the New York Rangers was the winner of the trophy in 1967.

14 On June 10th, 1970, Sam Pollock traded Ernie Hicke and a first round draft choice in the 1971 Entry Draft to the Oakland Seals for Francois Lacombe, cash and the Seals' first pick in the 1971 Draft. The Seals would finish last in the NHL in 1970-71, allowing the Canadiens to select Lafleur with the first overall selection in the 1971 Draft.

15 Mel Hill of the Boston Bruins in 1939 and Maurice "Rocket" Richard of the Montreal Canadiens in 1951.

16 Sweden's Borje Salming of the Toronto Maple Leafs was named to the 1976-77 team, along with Larry Robinson of the Montreal Canadiens.

QUIZ 63 ANSWERS

1 In the 2003-04 season, Brian Boucher of the Phoenix Coyotes went 332:01 without allowing a goal. Boucher would record 5 straight shutouts during his incredible streak.

2 Phil Esposito led the NHL in scoring in 1970-71 with 152 points followed by teammates Bobby Orr with 139, John Bucyk with 116 and Ken Hodge with 105.

3 MVP Vincent Lecavalier's superb play led Canada to the gold medal in 2004 World Cup of Hockey.

4 Red Kelly, coach of the Toronto Maple Leafs, felt that pyramids were a source of power and strength. Kelly placed small pyramids in the Leafs dressing room and under the player's bench for a 1976 Stanley Cup Quarter-Finals series versus the Philadelphia Flyers. "Pyramid Power" failed the Leafs as they dropped the series to the Flyers four games to three.

5 Rookie Bill Mosienko of the Chicago Blackhawks scored 32 goals and added 38 assists for 70 points in 1943-44.

6 Although Steve "Stumpy" Thomas was short in stature, his passion for the game of hockey allowed him to score over 400 NHL goals during his lengthy career.

7 The incomparable Wayne Gretzky was named the greatest hockey player of the 20th century.

8 Dick Irvin of the Montreal Canadiens inscribed poet John McCrae's famous words from the poem "In Flanders Fields" along the dressing room wall of "Les Glorieux".